Gender and Economic Growth in Kenya

Gender and Economic Growth in Kenya

Unleashing the Power of Women

Amanda Ellis

Jozefina Cutura

Nouma Dione

Ian Gillson

Clare Manuel

Judy Thongori

 THE WORLD BANK

ISBN-10: 0-8213-6919-9
ISBN-13: 978-0-8213-6919-7
eISBN-10: 0-8213-6920-2
eISBN-13: 978-0-8213-6920-3
DOI: 10.1596/978-0-8213-6919-7

Cover photo: Fabric design by Flotea Massawe, female entrepreneur.
Cover design by Drew Fasick, Serif Design Group.

The World Bank is committed to preserving endangered forests and natural resources. The Office of the Publisher has chosen to print *Gender and Economic Growth in Kenya* on recycled paper with 30 percent postconsumer fiber in accordance with the recommended standards for paper usage set by the Green Press Initiative, a nonprofit program supporting publishers in using fiber that is not sourced from endangered forests. For more information, visit www.greenpressinitiative.org.

Library of Congress Cataloging-in-Publication Data

World Bank.
   Gender and economic growth in Kenya : unleashing the power of women.
   p. cm.
   Includes bibliographical references.
   ISBN-13: 978-0-8213-6919-7
   ISBN-10: 0-8213-6919-9
   ISBN-10: 0-8213-6920-2 (electronic)
   1. Women—Kenya—Economic conditions. 2. Women in development—Kenya. I. Title.

HQ1381.W665 2007
330.967620082—dc22

2006039772

Contents

Boxes

Figures

Tables

Foreword

Throughout Africa, women are a powerful force for growth and development, making important contributions to the economy as workers and entrepreneurs, and to the welfare of their families. In many African countries, however, unequal access to property, discrimination in the labor market, and business-related obstacles hinder women from contributing even more to their countries' growth and well-being. Removing such obstacles can help not only to empower women, but also to unlock the full economic potential of their nations.

Gender and Economic Growth in Kenya was carried out at the request of Kenya's Ministry of Trade and Marketing, as the government was concerned that the challenges facing women entrepreneurs had not been adequately reflected in existing work on Kenya's investment climate. Building on the 2004 Foreign Investment and Advisory Service (FIAS) report "Improving the Commercial Legal Framework and Removing Administrative and Regulatory Barriers to Investment" and on the 2004 Strategic Country Gender Assessment prepared by the World Bank, the book looks at the legal and administrative barriers facing women in Kenya that limit their contribution to the economy. The authors find that Kenya's economic growth potential can be boosted by enabling women to contribute more fully and more effectively to the country's

Economic Recovery Strategy for Wealth and Employment Creation. *Gender and Economic Growth in Kenya* makes practical recommendations to address the obstacles identified. A complementary *Voices of Women Entrepreneurs in Kenya* publication profiles successful women business owners as role models and offers a unique perspective, grounded in experience, on the obstacles and constraints they have had to overcome.

The two reports were formally launched in Nairobi in May 2006 in the presence of nearly 100 businesswomen and businessmen, government officials, donors, and civil society representatives, whose continued active involvement will be essential if the assessment's practical recommendations are to be translated into action. The launch events included advocacy training for women entrepreneurs and a subregional training event on gender and economics. Following the launch, the findings of *Gender and Economic Growth in Kenya* were fully incorporated into the country's Private Sector Development Strategy.

The World Bank Group recognizes the importance of women's critical contribution to economic growth, especially in Africa. Through its new Gender Action Plan, which focuses on "gender equality as smart economics," the Bank is committed to act. For its part, the Africa Region is giving renewed attention to women's economic empowerment as a core element of its response to the Region's challenges. *Gender and Economic Growth in Kenya*, along with other studies in this series (Uganda 2006, Tanzania 2007), is a practical result of that commitment. Tackling the gender-based obstacles to entrepreneurship analyzed in this report will not only enable women in Kenya to make a fuller contribution to the economy and improve their families' livelihoods, but also help to create a business environment that is better for all enterprises in Kenya.

John Page
Chief Economist, Africa Region
World Bank

Acknowledgments

At the request of the Permanent Secretary of Kenya's Ministry of Trade and Industry, this report was prepared by a team led by Amanda Ellis and comprising Jozefina Cutura, Nouma Dione, Ian Gillson, Clare Manuel, and Judy Thongori.

Helpful comments were received from Mark Blackden, Matilde Bordon, Vyjayanti Desai, and Nyambura Githagui of the World Bank; Natalie Africa, Khetsiwe Dlamini, Peter Ladergaard, Vincent Palmade, and Roy Pepper of the IFC; Leila Mokaddem of the African Development Bank; and Simone Elouch of CIDA. Overall supervision for the gender and growth and trade chapters was provided by Helene Carlsson Rex and Andrew Morrison of the World Bank's Gender and Development Group.

The assessment is the result of a broad consultative process and draws on numerous individual interviews and group meetings with public and private sector stakeholders. We thank the World Bank Country Office and the IFC SME Solutions Center in Kenya for helping arrange interviews and focus group discussions with key stakeholders during missions in November 2005 and March 2006.

We would like to thank David Nalo, Permanent Secretary in Kenya's Ministry of Trade and Industry; Colin Bruce, World Bank Country

Director; and Jean Philippe Prosper, IFC Country Manager, for their support throughout the project. Finally, we thank the Kenyan women entrepreneurs whose views and concerns have added a critical dimension to this report, plus the representatives of business associations, civil society groups, donors, and government who volunteered to take the lead on implementing each of the recommendations (the lead agency is indicated in bold in the matrix on page xxi).

Acronyms and Abbreviations

ACP	African, Caribbean, and Pacific
AfDB	African Development Bank
AGOA	(U.S.) African Growth and Opportunity Act
AMWIK	Association of Media Women in Kenya
CEDAW	Convention on the Elimination of All Forms of Discrimination against Women
DFID	(U.K.) Department for International Development
DLT	District Land Tribunal
EPZ	Export Processing Zone
EPZA	Export Processing Zones Authority
ERS	*Economic Recovery Strategy for Wealth and Employment Creation 2003–2007*
EU	European Union
FI	financial institution
FIAS	Foreign Investment and Advisory Service
FIDA	Federation of Women Lawyers
FSDT	Financial Sector Deepening Trust
FLSTAP	Financial and Legal Sector Technical Assistance Project
GDP	gross domestic product

GGA	Gender and Economic Growth Assessment
GJLOS	Governance, Justice, Law and Order Sector
GoK	Government of Kenya
GOWE	Growth-Oriented Women Entrepreneur
ICA	Investment Climate Assessment
ICJ	International Commission of Jurists
IDA	International Development Association
IFC	International Finance Corporation
KANU	Kenyan African National Union
KARI	Kenya Agricultural Research Institute
KEPSA	Kenya Private Sector Alliance
KIPPRA	Kenya Institute for Public Policy Research and Analysis
K Sh	Kenyan shilling(s)
KWFT	Kenya Women Finance Trust
KWJA	Kenyan Women Judges Association
LCB	Land Control Board
LRC	(Kenya) Law Reform Commission
LSK	Law Society of Kenya
MFI	microfinance institution
MDG	Millennium Development Goal
MoJCA	Ministry of Justice and Constitutional Affairs
MoTI	Ministry of Trade and Industry
MSEs	micro and small enterprises
MSMEs	micro, small, and medium enterprises
MTEF	medium-term expenditure framework
MWPA	Married Women's Property Act
NCLR	National Council of Law Reporting
NCHR	National Commission for Human Rights
NGO	nongovernmental organization
OWIT	Organization of Women in International Trade
PSD	private sector development
PSDS	Private Sector Development Strategy
RLA	Registration of Land Act
SACCO	savings and credit cooperative
SMEs	small and medium enterprises
TA	technical assistance
U.K.	United Kingdom
UNCTAD	United Nations Conference on Trade and Development
UNDP	United Nations Development Programme
U.S.	United States

USAID	United States Agency for International Development
UWSACCO	United Women's Savings and Credit Cooperative Society
WBA	women's business association
WBENC	Women's Business and Enterprise National Council
WTO	World Trade Organization

Overview

Gender inequality is a serious economic issue in Kenya. Addressing it will lead to improved outcomes not only for women themselves, but for families and the society as a whole.

—David Nalo, Permanent Secretary, Ministry of Trade and Industry

This report examines the legal, administrative, and regulatory barriers that are preventing women in Kenya from contributing fully to the Kenyan economy. Building on the 2004 Foreign Investment and Advisory Service (FIAS) report, "Improving the Commercial Legal Framework and Removing Administrative and Regulatory Barriers to Investment," this study looks at the bureaucratic barriers facing women in Kenya through a gender lens. The report makes specific recommendations to address gender-related barriers in the context of ongoing government and donor initiatives to encourage private sector development as the key driver of poverty reduction and economic growth, in line with Kenya's *Economic Recovery Strategy for Wealth and Employment Creation 2003–2007 (ERS)*. Addressing these constraints will not only allow women to make a full contribution to the economy but also improve their livelihoods and those of their families and help create a more enabling environment for all businesses in Kenya.

The Kenyan government has institutionalized its commitment to addressing gender inequalities by creating a National Commission on Gender and Development and a Ministry of Gender, Sports, Culture and Social Services in 2004, as well as initiating Gender Desks in various ministries. Kenya is today also one of only two African countries with an active local chapter of the Organization of Women in International Trade (OWIT) in the private sector. Indeed, encouragement from OWIT promoted the creation of the Gender Unit in the Ministry of Trade and Industry.

This report was prepared at the request of the Ministry of Trade and Industry, in conjunction with the *Voices of Women Entrepreneurs in Kenya* publication and a Gender Review of the World Bank Group's International Development Association's (IDA's) micro, small, and medium enterprises (MSMEs) project. The *ERS* recognizes that Kenyan women have unequal access to opportunities and assets and that this is the single greatest determinant of poverty for women. Though there is a severe lack of up-to-date sex-disaggregated statistics in Kenya, available data show that women are actively contributing economically, despite various gender-based constraints. Removing these could provide a significant boost to Kenya's economy. Examining the implications of gender-based inequality and addressing the linkages between gender and economic growth are critical for the following objectives.

Meeting the government of Kenya's 7 percent real GDP growth target. This report finds that eliminating gender-based inequalities in education and access to agricultural inputs could result in a one-off increase in as much as 4.3 percentage points of GDP growth, followed by a sustained year-on-year increase of 2.0 to 3.5 percentage points in GDP growth.

Increasing formal sector employment. The government of Kenya's *ERS* sets the target of creating 500,000 jobs annually. Yet the *ERS* predicts that only 12 percent of the 2,636,130 jobs expected to be created over the 2003–07 period will be in the formal sector. With an estimated 85 percent of female-owned businesses being in the informal (*jua kali*) sector and women owning 48 percent of MSMEs, addressing the barriers facing women will be essential for increasing formal sector employment.

Reducing poverty levels by at least 5 percentage points, as set out in the *ERS*. Women in Kenya are poorer than men, with 54 percent of rural and 63 percent of urban women and girls living below the poverty line (Government of Kenya 1997). The World Bank's Country Assistance Strategy recognizes that "women are more likely to be poor and vulnerable to adverse shocks than men" (World Bank 2004d).

Increasing agricultural productivity and exports. Although women in Kenya supply 70 percent of labor in the agricultural sector, they hold only about 1 percent of registered land titles, with 5 to 6 percent of registered titles held in joint names (World Bank 2004a). Women's limited ability to own land and property negatively affects their ability to participate in producer groups, receive cash remuneration for their labor, and benefit from agricultural extension services. Their contribution to Kenya's economic growth is constrained because insecure land rights can limit women from making the necessary investments into their land to increase its productivity and economic value.

Increasing access to finance. In a largely collateral-based banking system, women's lack of property rights restricts their ability to access formal financing and hence hinders business growth.

Reducing the high HIV/AIDS rate for women. The prevalence of HIV/AIDS in Kenya is higher for women than for men, with infection rates for females in the 15 to 19 age range being a staggering five times higher than for males (World Bank 2003a). The increasing number of widows and orphans resulting from the high number of HIV/AIDS cases has significantly increased both women's workload and their financial responsibilities and has impacted their ability to contribute to economic life in Kenya (USAID 2002).

Meeting the Millennium Development Goals (MDGs). Although gender equality is an MDG in its own right (MDG 3), increasing research indicates that gender equality is essential for meeting all of the MDGs (World Bank 2003b).

Summary of Key Findings

Kenyan women are making a large (although frequently "invisible") economic contribution, particularly in agriculture and the informal business sector, while men tend to dominate in the formal sector. More than 75 percent of women live in rural areas (ILO 2004), where they dominate the agricultural sector (floriculture, tea, coffee, vegetables, cereals, poultry, mangos, and oranges). Women in Kenya are also "time-poor" because of their dual roles in the household economy and the labor market. On average, women work longer hours (12.9 hours) compared with those of men (8.2 hours) (figure 1), yet they earn less because more of these hours are not remunerated (Saito, Mekonnen, and Spurling 1994).

Women make up nearly half of all MSMEs, but their businesses tend to be smaller, are less likely to grow, have less capital investment than

Figure 1. Women's Time Burden in Kenya

Source: Saito, Mekonnen, and Spurling 1994.

male-owned firms, and are twice as likely as male-owned firms to be operating from home. Female-owned MSMEs report only 57 percent of the income earned by their male counterparts, and their businesses generate 40 percent of total MSME employment (Government of Kenya 1999). The report argues that women in Kenya face more severe legal, regulatory, and administrative barriers to starting and running businesses than do their male counterparts and that reducing these would therefore disproportionately benefit women. Key findings include the following:

- Women's limited land ownership restricts their access to formal financing mechanisms and decreases their contribution to Kenya's economic growth.
- Although access to finance is an obstacle for all firms, women rated it as the single biggest constraint that is preventing them from growing their businesses. The prevalence of a collateral-based banking system and lack of a credit bureau that could capture women's excellent repayment rates in microfinance are key constraints.
- Women's businesses face more severe bureaucratic barriers. Female-owned MSMEs are less likely to register their businesses, and they perceive tax rates, tax administration, and customs as greater constraints to business growth than men do (figure 2).
- Although an accessible justice system is vital for business operations—for enforcing contracts, settling employment disputes, and providing a sound foundation for collateral-based lending—women in Kenya face particular obstacles when accessing justice.
- International trade has had a significant impact on gender equality in private sector development, particularly for export industries where

Figure 2. Women Perceive Taxes and Customs as Greater Constraints to Business Growth

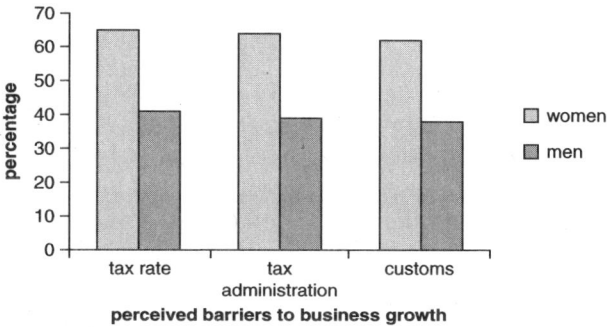

Source: World Bank 2006b.

the majority of employees are women, but it has also increased women's economic vulnerability. Women in Kenya constitute between 65 and 75 percent of workers in the cut flower sector, more than three-quarters of workers in the textiles sector, and about a third of the estimated workforce in tourism.

Synopsis of Each Section and Key Recommendations

Improving Access to Property Rights and Land
Land is vital both because of the predominance of agriculture within the Kenyan economy and because of the significance of land in providing collateral for business finance. Formal statute law potentially gives property rights to married women, and the 1882 Married Women's Property Act gives married women equal rights to own property. Furthermore, the Law of Succession Act gives women inheritance rights. However, the constitution exempts from its nondiscrimination provisions "members of a particular race or tribe" with respect to the application of their customary law. This exemption has a profound effect on the lives of many women in Kenya: for most of them, customary law is the only law to which they have recourse. The extent to which discriminatory customary law overrides largely nondiscriminatory statute law in relation to women's property rights has been a major source of judicial determination and is still an uncertain area of law. Moreover, for most women, the formal legal position is irrelevant in practice. For them, justice is dispensed at the local level, without recourse to the formal courts, and customary norms apply. In addition, formal registration practices and allocation of state land have

excluded women. Because women's interests are largely not noted on title deeds, the land on which they have customary user rights and on which they may depend for their livelihoods can be disposed of without their knowledge or consent.

Specific recommendations include the following:

- Through the government of Kenya's Governance, Justice, Law and Order Sector (GJLOS) Reform Programme, promulgate a training manual aimed at magistrates and customary leaders on women's property rights, setting out clearly case law that establishes that statute law on women's property rights prevails over discriminatory customary law.
- Monitor the impact of the training manual through considering property rights decisions at the local level (for example, market surveys undertaken by GJLOS).
- Strengthen the dissemination of knowledge about women's property rights and how women can enforce them (for example, through a radio soap, will-writing campaigns, and pamphlets such as the Federation of Women Lawyers' [FIDA's] "ABC of Property Law").
- Prioritize publication of law reports on women's property rights through GJLOS.
- Continue with training of Land Control Board (LCB) and District Land Tribunal (DLT) members in gender issues, and monitor impact at the local level (U.K. Department for International Development [DFID]).
- Nongovernmental organizations (NGOs) should continue to take strategic test cases to court to establish robust case law in relation to women's property rights.

Increasing Women's Access to Finance

Even though women entrepreneurs make up nearly half of all MSME owners, it is estimated that they have less than 10 percent of the available credit (Government of Kenya 1999) (figure 3). Kenya does not have a credit bureau that could capture women's excellent repayment histories, and products like leasing and factoring are not widely available. Even though microfinance is a great poverty reduction tool, it offers only limited support for women who wish to grow their enterprises beyond the micro level. Women business owners who have outgrown the maximum loan limits from microfinance institutions have great difficulties obtaining loans as small as Kenyan shillings (K Sh) 1 million from commercial banks.

Figure 3. Women's Access to Resources in Kenya

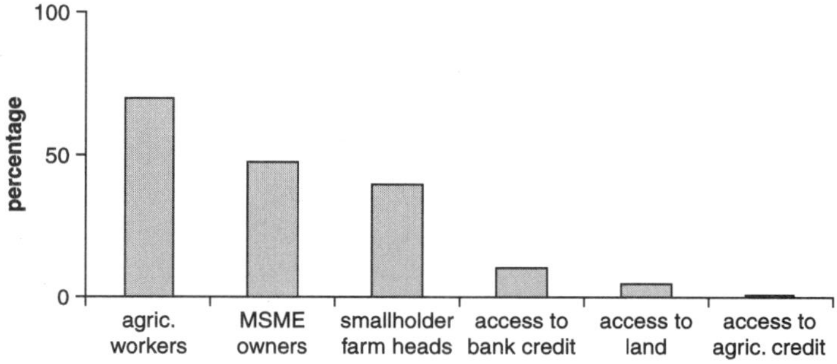

Source: Authors.

Recommendations for increasing women's access to finance include the following:

- Prioritize reform of part IV of the Companies Act, the Chattels Transfer Act, and common law in relation to movable property securities law by enacting a best-practice regime based on article 9 of the U.S. Uniform Commercial Code, as adapted for use in common law countries (for example, New Zealand).
- Collect and strengthen legislation to enable efficient exchange of credit information between financial institutions (FIs), especially between microfinance institutions (MFIs) and banks, leading to comprehensive coverage through a credit reference bureau.
- Encourage provision of financing mechanisms for female-owned businesses through local financial institutions and international development institutions.

Reducing Bureaucratic Barriers

Although the government of Kenya recognizes the importance of the MSME sector to job creation and economic growth, many women remain stuck running microenterprises in the informal sector. This Gender and Economic Growth Assessment (GGA) argues that there are specific legal, regulatory, and administrative barriers that women entrepreneurs face—that are either not encountered at all by their male counterparts or have a disproportionate effect on women. Because women tend to be "time-poor" (combining family duties with running their businesses) and have limited access to financial resources, they may be less likely to register their businesses. Yet evidence indicates that women may respond well to simplified registration procedures. Business licensing requirements are onerous, and a recent World Bank Urban Informal Sector Investment Climate Analysis in Kenya revealed that, on average, women perceive tax rates, tax administration, and customs to be greater constraints to business growth than men do (figure 2). Taxes and customs are costs of formalization, and this negative perception thus decreases the likelihood that women will register their businesses.

Specific recommendations for reducing bureaucratic barriers facing women include the following:

- Expedite the review of the overall steps for business registration, which is taking place under the World Bank IDA MSME Competitiveness project, with a view to simplifying the steps and associated costs, and develop a one-stop shop for business registration, business name registration, and other regulations.
- Expedite the process of replacing the Companies Act with a new regime based on international best practices in common law countries (for example, Australia, Canada, and New Zealand), in particular to streamline business entry procedures.
- The government must follow through on the steps and commitments already taken to implement the Business License Reform. In particular, the government must
  - assure that the required legal measures are submitted in a timely fashion to Parliament and receive legislative priority on the parliamentary agenda;
  - maintain a centralized and stringent application of the guillotine approach for the remaining 700 national government licenses and for all local government licenses; and
  - establish the Regulatory Review Unit and the Electronic Regulatory Registry, and ensure that appropriate mechanisms are in place to screen new business licenses and, at a later stage, other business regulation.

Improving Access to Justice

Formal courts in Kenya are generally too costly, time-consuming, complex, and geographically inaccessible for many Kenyans, particularly those in rural areas. Government-led reform efforts are under way, including the launch of the GJLOS Reform Programme in November 2003, which aims to fundamentally reform justice delivery in Kenya. A key GJLOS priority is to further strengthen the legal and policy framework in Kenya by removing gender-biased discriminatory legislation, policies, and regulations and to promote gender-sensitive, pro-poor laws, policies, and regulations that afford other vulnerable groups—and women in particular—their rightful place as equal participants in society through effective policy implementation.

Specific recommendations for increasing access to justice include the following:

- Strengthen gender mainstreaming within the GJLOS Reform Programme (implementation led by the Ministry of Justice and Constitutional Affairs), including the following:
  - Strengthen training for judges, magistrates, chiefs, and police on laws relating to women's property rights and women's rights in general and their responsibility to enforce those laws.
  - Publicize High Court decisions confirming women's inheritance and property rights, and ensure they are applied in the Magistrates Courts through monitoring decisions on a "spot-check" basis.
  - Ensure that the GJLOS monitoring and evaluation system includes sex-disaggregated data to enable the impact of justice reforms on women to be assessed.

Increasing Benefits from International Trade and Reforming Labor Laws

The Kenyan Ministry of Trade and Industry is already demonstrating leadership in its commitment to recognizing the links between trade policy, equitable growth, and gender issues. International trade has had not only a positive impact on Kenya's economy but also a significant impact on gender equality, particularly for export industries where the majority of employees are women. Trade has increased female employment in the formal sector and improved working conditions. Yet the booming international trade has also increased women's economic vulnerability. Factors such as outdated labor laws, as well as discrimination, lower skills, and gender inequalities in access to resources, have affected women's ability to fully benefit from the opportunities of increased trade.

Recommendations for reforming labor laws and increasing benefits from international trade for women include the following:

- The Central Bureau of Statistics, the Ministry of Trade and Industry, and the Ministry of Planning should enhance their collection and reporting of sex-disaggregated data to facilitate more detailed research into the impact of trade on gender relations and the livelihoods of women in Kenya.

- The Ministry of Trade and Industry should continue to strengthen its capacity to recognize the gender-differentiated impacts of trade liberalization and to ensure integration of systematic gender analysis in trade policy making and negotiations; continue to engage with women's business associations (WBAs) and civil society stakeholders to ensure their involvement in, and input to, Kenya's trade policy making and promotional efforts; and to promote gender awareness and social responsibility through appropriate engagement with the private sector.
- WBAs should ensure that they take the opportunity offered to be engaged and regularly interact with the Ministry of Trade and Industry, to increase their understanding of relevant issues.

The Way Forward

Following the formal launch of the GGA in May 2006, the assessment was accepted as an integral part of the government of Kenya's first Private Sector Development Strategy (PSDS), which sets out government's policy and medium-term priorities for achieving the objective of private sector-led growth in Kenya. A task force comprising representatives of the government of Kenya, civil society, donors, and the private sector has been convened to carry forward this work and translate the GGA's recommendations into tangible outcomes.

Matrix of Recommendations

Gender and Economic Growth Assessment in Kenya: Matrix of Recommendations

Issue	Recommendation	Responsibility	Suggested Impact/Priority
Gender and economic growth	Improve outreach of agricultural extension services to women	**Ministry of Agriculture, National Commission on Gender and Development (Gender Commission)**[a]	High/medium term
Land and property rights	Building on existing publications,[b] promulgate a training manual aimed at magistrates and customary leaders on women's property rights, setting out clearly case law that establishes that statute law on women's property rights prevails over discriminatory customary law	**Judiciary/Kenyan Association of Women Judges (KWJA),** Kenya Law Reform Commission (LRC), Gender Commission, National Council of Law Reporting (NCLR), Ministry of Justice and Constitutional Affairs (MoJCA)—GJLOS	High/immediate
	Monitor the impact of the training manual through considering property rights decisions at the local level (for example, market surveys)	**FIDA,** Ministry of Gender, Sports, Culture and Social Services (Ministry of Gender); National Commission for Human Rights (NCHR)	

(continued)

Gender and Economic Growth Assessment in Kenya: Matrix of Recommendations (*continued*)

Issue	Recommendation	Responsibility	Suggested Impact/Priority
Land and property rights	Strengthen the dissemination of knowledge about women's property rights and how women can enforce them (for example, through a radio soap, will-writing campaigns, and pamphlets such as FIDA's "ABC of Property Law")ᶜ	**FIDA,** MoJCA—GJLOS Ministry of Gender, Association of Media Women in Kenya (AMWIK), NCHR	High/immediate
Land and property rights	Prioritize publication of law reports on women's property rights	**NCLR,** MoJCA—GJLOS, KWJA, FIDA, AMWIK, Law Society of Kenya (LSK), NCHR	High/immediate
Land and property rights	Continue with training of Land Control Board and District Land Tribunal members in gender issues, and monitor impact at the local level	**U.K. Department for International Development (DFID),** MoJCA, Kenya School of Law	High/immediate
Land and property rights	Continue to take strategic test cases to court to establish robust case law in relation to women's property rights	**FIDA,** in cooperation with other NGOs	High/immediate
Land and property rights	Find an appropriate way to note women's user rights on the title (for example, as an easement or as an equitable interest under a trust)	**National Land Policy Secretariat, Ministry of Lands and Housing,** FIDA, NCHR, Kenya Land Alliance, IDA/MSME program, MoTI	High/immediate
Land and property rights	Encourage women's membership in cooperatives and access to cash remuneration through inclusion of names on land titles		
Land and property rights	Advocate for the gender recommendations in the "National Land Policy Issues and Recommendations Report"	**National Land Policy Secretariat, Kenya Land Alliance,** FIDA	Moderate/medium term
Land and property rights	Monitor allocation of state land for gender bias	**Ministry of Lands and Housing,** NCHR	Moderate/medium term

Land and property rights	Amend the Succession Act to eliminate discriminatory provisions	**FIDA, ICJ,** KWJA, Attorney General, LRC, Gender Commission, MoJCA, NCHR	Moderate/medium term
Land and property rights	Replace the U.K. Married Women's Property Act with a Kenyan statute, to include a presumption of spousal co-ownership of family property and equal division of family property upon separation or divorce	**LRC,** ICJ, FIDA, LSK, KWJA, MoJCA, NCHR	Moderate/medium term
Land and property rights	Require that all marriages be registered in the central registry, and expedite reorganization of the registry through the GJLOS	**LRC, Attorney General,** MoJCA—GJLOS, FIDA, ICJ, KWJA, NCHR, Gender Commission	Moderate/medium term
Access to finance and collateral	Prioritize reform of part IV of the Companies Act, the Chattels Transfer Act, and common law in relation to movable property securities law by enacting a best-practice regime based on article 9 of the U.S. Uniform Commercial Code, as adapted for use in common law countries (for example, New Zealand)	**Financial and Legal Sector Technical Assistance Project,** Kenya Bankers Association, LRC, Attorney General, Gender Commission	High/immediate
Access to finance and collateral	Collect and report sex-disaggregated data on the MSME sector by ensuring that future surveys and mapping exercises are gender-sensitive, and ensure that, in addition to the number of employees, the minimum financial need criteria are used to better profile MSMEs	**IDA MSME Project/USAID,** Central Bureau of Statistics	High/immediate

(continued)

Gender and Economic Growth Assessment in Kenya: Matrix of Recommendations (*continued*)

Issue	Recommendation	Responsibility	Suggested Impact/Priority
Access to finance and collateral	Collect and strengthen legislation to enable efficient exchange of credit information between financial institutions, especially between MFIs and banks, leading to comprehensive coverage through a credit reference bureau	**Central Bank of Kenya/IFC,** Kenya Bankers Association, Association of Microfinance Institutions, Ministry of Finance, FLSTAP, and WBAs, including the Organization of Women in International Trade (OWIT)	High/immediate
Access to the formal sector: business entry and licensing	Expedite the review of the overall steps for business registration, taking place under the World Bank IDA MSME Competitiveness project, with a view to simplifying the steps and associated costs, and develop a one-stop shop for business registration, business name registration, and other regulations	**MoJCA** – GJLOS/FLSTAP/LRC, Attorney General, MoTI **Registrar General's office, IDA MSME project,** Kenya Revenue Authority, FLSTAP, MoTI	High/immediate
Access to the formal sector: business entry and licensing	Expedite the process of replacing the Companies Act with a new regime based on international best practices in common law countries (for example, Australia, Canada, and New Zealand), in particular to streamline business entry procedures	**LRC, MoJCA – GJLOS,** FLSTAP, MoTI	High/immediate

Access to the formal sector: business entry and licensing	The government must follow through on the steps and commitments already taken to implement the Business License Reform. In particular, it must do the following: • Assure that the required legal measures are submitted in a timely fashion to Parliament and receive legislative priority on the parliamentary agenda • Maintain a centralized and stringent application of the guillotine approach for the remaining 700 national government licenses and for all local government licenses • Establish the Regulatory Review Unit and the Electronic Regulatory Registry, and ensure that appropriate mechanisms are in place to screen *new* business licenses and, at a later stage, other business regulation	**Ministry of Finance, FIAS, World Bank,** MoTI	High/immediate
Access to justice	Strengthen training for judges, magistrates, chiefs, and police in laws relating to women's property rights and to women's rights in general and their responsibility to enforce those laws	**Judiciary, KWJA,** FIDA, ICJ, AMWIK, LSK, LRC, Gender Commission, NCLR, MoJCA—GJLOS	High/immediate
Access to justice	Publicize High Court decisions confirming women's inheritance and property rights, and ensure that they are applied in the Magistrates Courts through monitoring decisions on a "spot-check" basis	**Judiciary,** AMWIK, FIDA, ICJ, LJK, NCLR, MoJCA—GJLOS	High/immediate
Access to justice	Ensure that the GJLOS monitoring and evaluation system includes sex-disaggregated data to enable impact of justice reforms on women to be assessed	**MoJCA—GJLOS**	High/immediate

(continued)

Gender and Economic Growth Assessment in Kenya: Matrix of Recommendations (*continued*)

Issue	Recommendation	Responsibility	Suggested Impact/Priority
Access to justice	Ensure that the proposed national legal aid system adequately addresses gender issues, strengthens community-based justice by equipping NGO community-based field workers with tools and techniques to mediate disputes in a gender-sensitive manner, and trains community leaders to do the same	**MoJCA—GJLOS,** FIDA, KWJA	Moderate/medium term
International trade	Enhance the collection and reporting of sex-disaggregated data to facilitate more detailed research into the impact of trade on gender relations and the livelihoods of women in Kenya	**Central Bureau of Statistics, MoTI,** Ministry of Planning	High/immediate
International trade	Continue to strengthen the capacity of MoTI to recognize the gender-differentiated impacts of trade liberalization and ensure integration of systematic gender analysis in trade policy making and negotiations; continue to engage with women's business associations (WBAs) and civil society stakeholders to ensure their involvement in, and input to, Kenya's trade policy making and promotional efforts; and promote gender awareness and social responsibility through appropriate engagement with the private sector	**MoTI Gender Unit,** IFC GEM, Comsec, World Bank	Moderate/medium term

Labor	Ensure that WBAs take the opportunity offered to be engaged and regularly interact with MoTI to increase their understanding of relevant issues Facilitate capacity building of MoTI officials and WBAs on the linkages between international trade and gender and on the practical tools available to assist women entrepreneurs in accessing trade-related information and training	**Ministry of Labour and Human Resource Development,** MoTI	Moderate/medium term
Labor	Undertake regulatory impact assessments on proposed new labor laws, including a gender assessment, and ensure that the proposed new maternity provisions will not have the unintended consequence of excluding women from the workplace Make efforts to upgrade skills for women's MSMEs Offer training and capacity building for export-oriented women entrepreneurs, and review the industrial training levy scheme	**Ministry of Labour and Human Resource Development, Ministry of Education** MoTI Gender Unit, Kenya Institute of Business Training, IDA MSME project, AfDB GOWE project	Moderate/medium term
Private sector development strategy	Strengthen the developing Private Sector Development Strategy (PSD) in the following ways: • Include a clearly articulated policy statement in relation to government's role in enabling private sector–led growth in general, and create the environment to enhance women's role in achieving it in particular	**MoTI, PSD Donor Group,** Ministry of Gender, Ministry of Planning, KEPSA, Kenya Association of Manufacturers	High/immediate

(continued)

Gender and Economic Growth Assessment in Kenya: Matrix of Recommendations *(continued)*

Issue	Recommendation	Responsibility	Suggested Impact/Priority
	• Map the government of Kenya's ongoing private sector development (PSD) initiatives, including those relating to women, and develop an holistic framework for implementing them, including implementation structures and a monitoring and evaluation framework		
	• Identify gaps not covered by current initiatives, such as the issues addressed by this GGA		
	• In relation to each PSDS goal, consider gender-related barriers to achieving that goal and address them (for example, in the section on access to capital in the current document, the issue of women's limited access to capital is not discussed at all)		
	• Ensure that the PSDS implementation arrangements, insofar as they involve the private sector, include representation from women entrepreneurs or groups representing them		
	• Design the monitoring and evaluation arrangements for the Strategy to ensure that data are sex-disaggregated		
Advocacy	Work to strengthen women's businesses associations to better advocate for needed change, including those identified in this GGA	**AFDB GOWE, KEPSA,** WBAs, including OWIT and the Kenya Women Entrepreneurs Board	High/immediate

| Advocacy | Provide the Gender Commission with the needed capacity and authority for effective implementation of its mandate and enable it to truly become an effective coordinating and advocacy body, including in relation to the gender dimensions of private sector issues | **Ministry of Gender, Gender Donor Roundtable** | Moderate/medium term |

Source: Authors' findings.

a. Bold letters indicate the lead agency.

b. NGOs have published excellent guides, including the Education Centre for Women in Democracy's field guide: *Succession and Inheritance in Kenya: A Handbook for Paralegals and Wananchi.* FIDA has produced "ABC of Property Law."

c. The "ABC of Property Law" needs to be updated and printed.

CHAPTER 1

Overview of Kenya's Legal Framework

Under the current constitution, {it seems} a woman can be discriminated against and it is not against the law.

—Mary Okello, Makini Schools, *Voices of Women Entrepreneurs in Kenya*

How Does Kenya's Legal Framework Impact on Gender Issues?

This report argues that women in Kenya face more severe legal, regulatory, and administrative barriers to starting and running businesses than do their male counterparts. To what extent is this gender inequality the result of deficiencies in Kenya's legal framework?

Although Kenya has committed to gender equality through international law and is party to many key international conventions on the status of women (table 1.1), including the important Convention for the Elimination of All Forms of Discrimination against Women (CEDAW), this has not translated into domestic law.

International Obligations Have Impacted Little on Domestic Law

At the 1985 World Conference of Women held in Nairobi, the domestication of CEDAW was seen as an important step toward implementation

Table 1.1. International Treaties on Women's Rights

International agreement	Ratifications
Convention for the Suppression of the Traffic in Persons and of the Exploitation of the Prostitution of Others (1949)	Not ratified
Convention on the Political Rights of Women (1952)	Not ratified
Convention on the Nationality of Married Women (1957)	Not ratified
Convention on Consent to Marriage, Minimum Age for Marriage, and Registration of Marriages (1962)	Not ratified
The International Covenant on Civil and Political Rights (1966)	Ratified
The International Covenant on Economic, Social, and Cultural Rights (1966)	Ratified
Optional Protocol to the International Covenant on Civil and Political Rights (1966)	Not ratified
Convention on the Elimination of All Forms of Discrimination against Women (1979)	Ratified
The African (Banjul) Charter on Human and People's Rights (African Charter) (1981)	Ratified
The Protocol to the African Charter on Human and People's Rights on the Rights of Women in Africa (2003)	Not ratified

Source: Owuor 1999.

of the basic rights for women. But Kenyan domestic law has not been amended to comply with the Convention in a number of important respects, particularly in relation to succession and matrimonial law. Kenya does not have an automatic domestication clause in respect to ratified international conventions, and so domestication of Kenya's international obligations has to be undertaken through reforming individual pieces of legislation. This has not been done.

Kenya's Constitution Entrenches Gender Inequality

At the time of writing, Kenyans have just rejected a proposed new constitution, which included the right to equal opportunities in political, social, and economic activities for men and women in the Bill of Rights section, as well as equal rights to inherit and own property. Kenya's existing constitution largely dates from its independence from the United Kingdom (U.K.) in 1963. It asserts—in Articles 70 and 82(1)—that there should be no discrimination before the law in the treatment of different persons (box 1.1).

But there is tension in the constitution between the principle of nondiscrimination and the various constitutional exemptions to it. A government task force appointed to review the laws relating to women

(Owuor 1999) summarized the very significant exemptions, as shown in table 1.2.

The impact of these constitutional provisions can be seen in some of Kenya's key laws that go to the heart of gender inequality.

Box 1.1

The Constitution Appears to Provide for Equality

... every person in Kenya is entitled to the fundamental rights and freedoms of the individual, that is to say, the right, whatever his . . . creed or sex . . . , to each and all of the following, namely—

(a) life, liberty, security of the person and the protection of the law;
(b) freedom of conscience, of expression and of assembly and association; and
(c) protection for the privacy of his home and other property and from deprivation of property without compensation

Article 70

Discrimination is defined *in subsection 3* to include—

affording different treatment to different persons attributable wholly or mainly to their respective descriptions by race, . . . sex, whereby persons of one such description are subjected to disabilities or restrictions to which persons of another such description are not made subject or are accorded privileges or advantages which are not accorded to persons of another such description

Article 82(1)

Table 1.2. Significant Exceptions to the Equality Provisions

Article	Content of exception
82(4)	• Nondiscrimination does not apply in relation to citizenship issues.
82(5)	• Nondiscrimination does not apply to a law that deals with adoption, marriage, divorce, burial, inheritance, or other matters of personal law nor to "members of a particular race or tribe" with respect to the application of their customary law.
82(5)	• Nondiscrimination does not apply to a statute that prescribes standards regarding appointment to an office in the public service, in a disciplined force, in local authority service, or in the public body corporate.
82(6)	• Nondiscrimination does not apply to the giving or withholding of consent to a transaction in agricultural land by any body established by law for the control of such transactions.

Source: Owuor 1999.

Kenya's Statutory Legislation Reflects This Discriminatory Framework

Various statutes in Kenya reflect this discriminatory framework entrenched in the constitution. Some examples are given in box 1.2.

The Constitution Permits Discriminatory Customary Law Practices

The constitution exempts from its nondiscrimination provisions "members of a particular race or tribe" with respect to the application of their customary law. This exemption has a profound effect on the lives of many women in Kenya: for most of them, customary law is the only law to which they have recourse.

Kenya has about 40 indigenous ethnic groups, with variations of customary laws among the different ethnic groups, and even at the clan and family levels. Although each system is different and few are written, general principles that apply across most systems can be ascertained. In general, customary law systems are based on patriarchal traditions in

---

Box 1.2

Discriminatory Statutes

Law of Succession Act
- A widow's (but not widower's) inheritance rights are terminated upon remarriage.
- A father's rights are prioritized before a mother's in intestate succession.

The Divorce Laws
- A man who succeeds in a divorce petition on the grounds of the adultery of his wife is entitled to damages against the corespondent, while a wife who succeeds in similar circumstances is not entitled to damages, but can get only costs.

The Children's Act 2001
- Women are responsible for children born outside marriage, while a man is not automatically responsible for his children born outside marriage. It is only where the man has acknowledged the child, maintained the child, cohabited with the child's mother for 12 months after the child is born, or accepted parental responsibility that he is required to have responsibility over the child.[a]

a. Sections 24(3) and 25.

which the principal decision-making power is allocated to men, and men inherit and control land and property (box 1.3).

Customary law is enforced by traditional leaders (such as elders) and local authorities (such as government-appointed chiefs), but customary law may also be applied in the formal courts by judges and magistrates. The Judicature Act[1] provides that a formal court's jurisdiction must be exercised in conformity with the constitution (which allows for discrimination based on customary law), statutes, and other sources of formal law. The Act states that the courts should be guided by customary law so far as it is "applicable and is not repugnant to justice and morality or inconsistent with any written law."

The extent to which discriminatory customary law overrides largely nondiscriminatory statute law in relation to women's property rights has been a major source of judicial determination and is still an uncertain area of law. But for most women, the formal legal position is irrelevant in practice. For them, justice is dispensed at the local level, without recourse to the formal courts, and customary norms apply.

Box 1.3

Broad Principles of Customary Laws in Kenya

- Married women do not inherit from their parents.
- Unmarried women inherit less from their parents than their brothers do.
- Women with sons may retain their husbands' property, but only to hold it in trust for the sons.
- Women with no children or with daughters are not likely to inherit from their husbands, and the estate is given to male relatives as if she were unmarried.
- Divorced or separated women are expected to leave the matrimonial home and return to their parents with only personal items.
- Unmarried daughters can use land in the paternal household, but only for certain crops.
- Married women have less control over significant family property than men do.
- Usually property that a wife acquires before and during a marriage is controlled and essentially owned by the husband.
- In some communities, the hut that a widow shared with her husband is destroyed after his death, and she is built a new (and often inferior) hut after she is cleansed or inherited.

Source: Human Rights Watch 2003.

Government Recognizes the Need to Address These Barriers

To take forward the growth-oriented policies in the *Economic Recovery Strategy for Wealth and Employment Creation 2003–2007 (ERS)*, the Ministry of Trade and Industry has developed Kenya's first Private Sector Development Strategy (PSDS). The PSDS document sets out the government's medium-term priorities to enable private sector–led growth in Kenya, and it recognizes gender as a "crosscutting issue" that must be integrated within the government policies. In addition (as discussed in chapter 8), following encouragement from the Organization of Women in International Trade, the Ministry of Trade and Industry established a Gender Desk in 2004 to ensure gender mainstreaming within the Ministry. Given the increasing amount of research that demonstrates the importance of reducing gender inequalities for economic growth and poverty reduction, these are steps in a positive direction.

Input into the Private Sector Development Strategy and Other Initiatives

This Gender and Economic Growth Assessment (GGA) is designed to feed into the development and the implementation of the PSDS. It makes specific recommendations for legal, regulatory, and administrative reform that will significantly impact on the ability of Kenyan women to start and grow their businesses. It is recommended that these be adopted by the government of Kenya as part of the PSDS. Recommendations are also made throughout the study in relation to Kenya's ongoing Governance, Justice, Law, and Order Sector Reform Programme and other projects, such as the World Bank/DFID Financial and Legal Technical Assistance Project and the IDA MSME project, as well as the government of Kenya's *Economic Recovery Strategy for Wealth and Employment Creation 2003–2007* and the recently created National Commission on Gender and Development.

The GGA begins with an overview of the legal framework, followed by an analysis of the nexus between gender and economic growth, arguing in chapter 2 that reducing gender inequality could have a significant impact on Kenya's economic growth. Chapter 3 focuses on property rights and access to land. Chapter 4 considers the related and vital issue of the very limited access to collateral—and thus to finance—faced by many female-owned businesses in Kenya. Chapter 5 considers the barriers that lie in the way of women who wish to make the transition from the informal to the formal sector and realize potential for greater growth. Having considered specific areas where women face legal, regulatory, and administrative discrimination, chapter 6 examines gender inequalities in access to justice. Chapter 7 looks at the differential opportunities and impact of international trade on men and women. Finally, the last chapter (8) discusses the institutional framework and Kenya's ongoing reform processes for implementing the recommendations presented in this assessment.

In each case, specific policy recommendations are made about how to address the barriers, and chapter 8 presents a way forward for integrating these recommendations into government's ongoing reform initiatives, notably the PSDS.

Note

1. Chapter (Cap.) 8, Laws of Kenya.

CHAPTER 2

The Gender/Economic Growth Nexus

Gender inequality is a serious economic issue in Kenya. Addressing it will lead to improved outcomes not only for women themselves, but for families and the society as a whole.

—David Nalo, Permanent Secretary, Ministry of Trade and Industry

There is growing recognition internationally that gender equality is good for economic growth and essential for poverty reduction (Ellis 2004). Where gender inequalities constitute barriers to women entering or participating fully in markets, economic growth and private sector development will be constrained with less investment, less competition, and lower productivity (Blackden and Bhanu 1999). Gender inequalities can also adversely affect the outcome of trade and macroeconomic policy reforms and their ability to translate incentives into economic development.

Although the government of Kenya's *Economic Recovery Strategy for Wealth and Employment Creation 2003–2007* recognizes that women have unequal access to opportunities and assets, it does not examine the implications of this inequality (Government of Kenya 2003a). Studies elsewhere have shown that these inequalities are worth considering. For example, World Bank research indicates that if the Middle East and North Africa region had introduced the same policies as East Asia with regard to gender equality in access to education and employment, it could have grown 0.7 percent faster per year during the 1990s—equivalent to US$424 billion. If women had worked outside the home, this growth could have translated into a 20–25 percent increase in net family income (World Bank 2003d). Research in Uganda suggests that the country could gain up to 2 percentage points of gross domestic product (GDP) growth a year by addressing gender-based inequalities in education and formal sector employment (World Bank 2004a).

For Kenya, Klasen (2002) shows that the fact that women during the 1960–92 period did not complete as many years of schooling on average as men did accounts for almost 1 percentage point difference between the long-run growth potential of Kenya when compared with that of high-performing Asian economies (with long-run growth rates of 4.5 percent). Moreover, Quisumbing (1996) estimates that increasing female access to agricultural inputs to the same level as that of their male counterparts would increase yields by 22 percent (appendix 1). In Kenya, economic analysis therefore suggests that eliminating gender-based inequalities in education and access to agricultural inputs could result in a one-off increase in output by as much as 4.3 percentage points of GDP, followed by a sustained year-on-year increase of 2.0 to 3.5 percentage points in GDP growth.

Women Start from a Disadvantaged Position

The starting point for this analysis is an overview of the position of women in Kenyan society (table 2.1).

Women in Kenya are poorer than men. Kenya's national poverty rate[1] was 53 percent in 2005. The World Bank's Country Assistance Strategy recognizes that "women are more likely than men to be poor, and [more] vulnerable to adverse shocks than men" (World Bank 2004d). In Kenya, 54 percent of rural and 63 percent of urban women and girls live below the poverty line (Government of Kenya 1997).

Women Predominate in Agriculture, but Their Contribution Tends to be Unpaid

The agricultural sector in Kenya has been the mainstay of the economy, accounting for 24 percent of GDP, more than 50 percent of total export revenues, and 62 percent of overall employment. Women are a major force in the agricultural sector (floriculture, tea, coffee, vegetables, cereals,

Table 2.1. Gender Profile of Kenya

	Female	Male
Population (1000s), 2004	18,958	18,111
Headed households (%), 1999	36.7	63.3
Fertility rate (avg. no. of children per woman), 2003	4.8	..
Life expectancy (years), 1999	60.4	52.8
Unemployment rate (%), 2004	11.9	8.4
Gross primary school enrollment ratio,[a] 2004	102	108
Net primary school enrollment ratio,[b] 2000–04	84	86
Primary completion rate, 2004		56[c]
Illiteracy rate (%), 2002	21.5	10.0
Transition rates from primary to secondary schools (%), 2004	44.3	47.1

Source: Adapted from Government of Kenya (2005b).
a. The gross enrollment ratio is the number of students enrolled in a level of education, whether or not they belong in the relevant age group for that level, as a percentage of the population in the relevant age group for that level.
b. Net enrollment is the number of students enrolled in a level of education who belong in the relevant age group, as a percentage of the population in that age group.
c. This figure combines statistics for both genders.

poultry, mangos, and oranges). They constitute more than 70 percent of all agricultural workers,[2] but frequently operate on an unpaid family basis (Government of Kenya 2000b). The latest available data indicate that women provide more than 80 percent of the labor in food production and 50 percent in cash crop production (Curry, Kooijman, and Recke 1999), specifically for cultivation, marketing, and agroprocessing (Horenstein 1989). Women are also increasingly becoming farm managers and heads of farm households, with estimates that more than 40 percent of all smallholder farms in Kenya are managed by women (Kimenye 1999). Yet women hold only about 1 percent of registered land titles in Kenya (5–6 percent of registered titles are held in joint names). Without title deeds, women are often unable to access cooperative membership, markets, and credit.

Although the Kenya government's Agricultural Productivity Project has aimed to increase agricultural production and improve farming methods, men control most of the resources for, and proceeds from, the sector. Thus, although women in Kenya have the potential to become more efficient, they lack the complementary inputs that would increase their productivity. Female-headed farms own, on average, less than half of the capital equipment owned by male-headed farms (World Bank 2001). In particular, the lack of appropriate small-scale technology for processing and storage has been found to be a major limitation for female farmers in Kenya (USAID 2002).

In the agricultural sector, training and extension services and the use of female field extension workers are important factors in raising female productivity (Quisumbing 1996). However, the FAO estimates that only 7 percent of agricultural extension services in Africa are directed toward female farmers and only about 11 percent of all extension personnel are women (FAO 1989). In Kenya, women typically receive less than 10 percent of the credit awarded to smallholders and only 1 percent of the total amount of credit directed to agriculture (FAO 1998).

Women Are Less Predominant in Formal Sector Employment and Tend to Have Lower Wages

Although women are major actors in Kenya's economy, particularly in agriculture and the informal business sector, men tend to dominate in the formal sector. Most women (58 percent) in the formal sector are employed in service industries, mainly education (table 2.2), and they typically occupy the lower-paid jobs (Manda 2002). But the labor market is changing: higher-skilled women are increasingly being employed—including at senior levels—in high-growth sectors such as telecoms and mobile phones.

Table 2.2. Formal Sector Employment in Kenya by Industry and Sex, 2004

	Males		Females		Total
	(000s)	% of total	(000s)	% of total	(000s)
Agriculture & forestry	241.0	75	79.6	25	320.6
Mining & quarrying	4.3	78	1.2	22	5.5
Manufacturing	199.8	83	42.2	17	242.0
Electricity & water	17.1	82	3.8	18	20.9
Building & construction	72.4	94	4.9	6	77.3
Trade, restaurants, & hotels	123.0	73	45.0	27	168.0
Transport & communications	78.4	80	19.9	20	98.3
Finance, insurance, real estate, & business services	63.1	74	22.1	26	85.2
Community, social, & personal services *of which*:	443.3	59	302.6	41	745.9
Public administration	95.7	63	56.5	37	152.2
Education services	188.1	57	143.3	43	331.4
Domestic services	59.8	60	39.6	40	99.4
Other services	99.7	61	63.2	39	162.9
Total *of which*:	**1,242.4**	**70**	**521.3**	**30**	**1,763.7**
Regular	995.8	72	394.7	28	1,390.5
Casual	246.6	66	126.6	34	373.2

Source: Government of Kenya 2005a.

Kenyan Women Constitute Almost Half of Micro and Small Business Owners

Women are major actors in the informal sector of the Kenyan economy. Although current sex-disaggregated data are not available, the government of Kenya's most recent statistics indicate that women own almost half (48 percent) of the 1.3 million micro-, small-, and medium-size enterprises (MSMEs) in Kenya (table 2.3). Even though a significant 85 percent of female-owned MSMEs are in the informal sector and two-thirds are located in rural areas, the average MSME generates a gross income equivalent to more than twice the average minimum wage in the agricultural sector (US$76 per month). It is estimated that MSMEs generate as much as 20 percent of Kenya's GDP (Government of Kenya 2006b); however, female-owned MSMEs report only 57 percent of the income earned by their male counterparts. They also have fewer employees: the average number of employees in a female-owned MSME is 1.54, compared with 2.1 for a male-owned MSME. As a result, 60 percent of total MSME employment is generated by male-owned and 40 percent by female-owned MSMEs (box 2.1) (Government of Kenya 1999).

Women's Dual Roles and Time Burden Affect Economic Productivity

Employment and national accounts data do not capture nonmarket activities (where women predominate) and therefore fail to demonstrate the full contribution of women to the household economy and the extent of the female work burden. Women in Kenya are "time-poor" because of their dual roles in the household economy[3] and the labor market. On average, women work longer hours (12.9 hours) compared

Table 2.3. Ownership and Location of MSMEs in Kenya

Location	Male-owned MSMEs		Female-owned MSMEs		Total MSMEs	
	No. of firms	Total employment	No. of firms	Total employment	No. of firms	Total employment
Urban	213,262	470,380	227,886	338,940	441,148	809,320
	(48.3%)	(58.1%)	(51.7%)	(41.9%)	(100%)	(100%)
Rural	457,465	944,270	384,961	607,660	842,427	1,551,930
	(54.3%)	(60.8%)	(45.7%)	(39.2%)	(100%)	(100%)
Total	670,727	1,414,650	612,847	946,600	1,283,575	2,361,250
	(52.3%)	(59.9%)	(47.7%)	(40.1%)	(100%)	(100%)

Source: Adapted from Government of Kenya (1999).

Box 2.1

Women's Businesses Differ from Men's

- Involved in different sectors, owning the majority of enterprises in food processing, clothing, agroprocessing, horticultural, and food preparation sectors. (Seventy-five percent of enterprises headed by women are in the trade and service sectors.)[a]
- Smaller: More than 85 percent of enterprises owned by women do not have any employees apart from the owner.
- Less likely to grow: Male-headed firms are estimated to grow on average by 11 percent a year, compared with 7 percent for female-headed firms.
- Founded on less capital investment than male-owned firms are.
- Twice as likely as male-owned firms to be operating from home.

Source: McCormick 2001.
a. Government of Kenya 2005e.

Figure 2.1. Women's Time Burden in Kenya

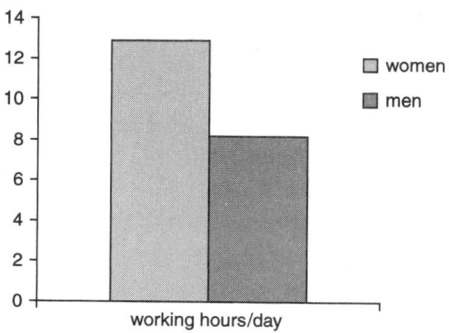

working hours/day

Source: Saito, Mekonnen, and Spurling 1994.

with those of men (8.2 hours), yet women earn less because more of these hours are not remunerated (figure 2.1) (Saito and Spurling 1994). Women constitute 60.8 percent of unpaid family workers.

Women in rural areas of Kenya are burdened with household tasks, such as collecting firewood and pounding grain. Only 30 percent of households in Kenya have access to piped water supplies, and fetching water can account for up to 40 percent of a woman's day, taking from 3 to 5.25 hours (Were and Kiringai 2003). Childcare is also an important source of time burden for women in Kenya. Women's labor time and flexibility are therefore more constrained than men's. The disproportionate cost borne by women in terms of reproductive work in the household economy limits the time that they can spend on economic activities and means that they may have less time to devote to developing their businesses (Blackden and Morris-Hughes 1993). The 2006 World Bank Country Social Analysis argues that women's burdens in the economic, domestic, and collective spheres have only intensified, bringing about a destabilizing effect on households and leading increasingly to tension and violence (World Bank 2006c).

Women Are Particularly Impacted by HIV/AIDS and Are Victims of Gender-Related Violence

The prevalence of HIV/AIDS in Kenya is higher for women than for men (figure 2.2), with infection rates for females in the 15 to 19 age range being a staggering five times higher than for males (World Bank 2004a). The increasing number of widows and orphans resulting from the high number of HIV/AIDS cases has significantly increased women's workload and their financial responsibilities (USAID 2002). Growing evidence indicates that gender-based violence contributes to the higher infection rates for women. Other reasons include traditional norms and

Figure 2.2. HIV Prevalence Rate, 2003

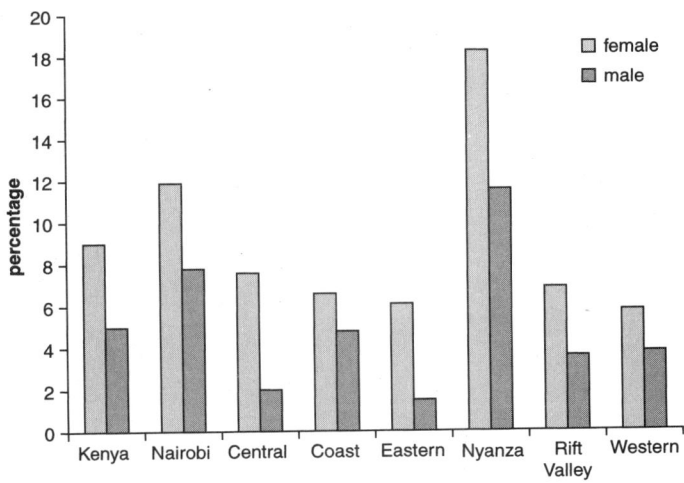

Source: Government of Kenya 2005b.

cultural practices, as well as women's economic dependence on men (World Bank 2004a). HIV/AIDS is also having an impact on already insecure land rights for women (box 2.2).

Moreover, physical and sexual violence commonly affects women and girls in Kenya. The World Bank Country Social Analysis notes that half of all Kenyan women have experienced violence since they were 15, and there has been a marked increase in violence and crime in recent years (World Bank 2006c). Cases of reported violence against women increased by 10 percent between 2003 and 2004 (Government of Kenya 2005a). The Kenyan Strategic Country Gender Assessment reports that 24 percent of women in the country have been victims of rape. Perpetrators are listed as male household staff, neighbors, ex-husbands, employers or supervisors, and landlords (World Bank 2004a). In 2002, 60 percent of married women in Kenya reported that they were victims of domestic violence, and 83 percent of women reported physical abuse in childhood, with more than 60 percent reporting physical abuse as adults (Johnston 2002a, 2002b). Under customary law, a man's beating his wife can be considered reasonable chastisement and may therefore take place with impunity. Gender-based abuse and violence clearly

---

Box 2.2

HIV/AIDS Is Undermining Land Tenure Security

HIV/AIDS has caused changes in land use, household labor, and financial standing because of loss of financial assets, higher costs of living with HIV/AIDS, increased burdens of caregiving and orphan fostering, and general disintegration of family ties. Research carried out in 2002 in rural sites in Embu, Thika, and Bondo districts suggested the following:

- HIV/AIDS creates a "missing generation," distorting inheritance and transmission patterns to grandchildren.
- Widows and their children can be vulnerable in terms of potential loss of land rights on the death of the male household head. Young widows were found to be more vulnerable than old ones.
- Distress sales of land resulting from HIV/AIDS were rare: sales are, if possible, avoided because the value of family land as a safety net is recognized. People are more likely to sell household assets to pay for medical and school fees.

Sources: World Bank 2003a; Strickland 2004.

inhibit women's ability to participate actively in public and economic life in Kenya.

Inequalities in Access to Education Have an Adverse Impact on Growth

Although gender inequalities in educational enrollment at the primary level have narrowed to almost parity following the introduction of free primary education in Kenya in 2003, disparities in secondary and university education persist and negatively affect both women's labor force participation and their ability to acquire the skills needed to start and grow a business (table 2.4). At the tertiary level, 63 percent of the students enrolled in 2004 were male, while only 37 percent were female, a gap that has not narrowed between 2000 and 2004. The cost of education is the most common cause for girls dropping out of school (Government of Kenya 2002). In general, when the cost of education increases at the household level, families tend to prefer schooling for boys. Factors such as teenage pregnancy and early marriages also lead to lower transition rates to secondary and tertiary education for girls (Kimalu et al. 2002). The World Bank Country Social Analysis notes that girls face a risk of sexual abuse on their way to and from school, as well as a greater burden of domestic tasks compared with that of boys when they arrive home (World Bank 2006c). Women's lower education levels result in their lower formal labor force participation, as well as higher fertility and lower levels of skills for women entrepreneurs.

A growing body of macroeconomic evidence shows that gender inequalities in access to schooling constrain productivity and output. Klasen uses education spending as a share of GDP, initial fertility levels,

Table 2.4. Education Enrollment by Gender, 2000–04

(000s) (% of total boys + girls)

	2000		2004	
	Boys	*Girls*	*Boys*	*Girls*
Primary	3,065	3,014	3,810	3,574
	(50%)	(50%)	(52%)	(48%)
Secondary	403	356	482	431
	(53%)	(47%)	(53%)	(47%)
University	37	22	58	34
	(63%)	(37%)	(63%)	(37%)

Source: Adapted from Government of Kenya (2005a).

and changes in these as instruments for levels of, and changes in, the female-to-male ratio of years of education. He concludes that gender inequalities have a significant and adverse impact on economic growth rates (Klasen 1999). For Kenya, Klasen shows that the fact that women during the 1960–92 period did not complete as many years of schooling on average as men did accounts for almost a percentage point difference between the long-run growth potential of Kenya when compared with those of high-performing Asian economies (Klasen 2002). Furthermore, private rates of return to additional schooling for women have been shown to be at least as large as those for men and often higher (Schultz 1991), implying potentially higher marginal returns of increased investment in female education in Kenya.

For secondary education, Dollar and Gatti, using a sample of more than 100 countries, found that an increase in 1 percentage point of the share of adult women with secondary schooling increases per capita income growth, on average, by 0.3 percentage point (Dollar and Gatti 1999). Applying the Dollar and Gatti results to Kenya would imply a year-on-year increase in GDP growth of 3.5 percentage points if female secondary education enrollment were brought up to the level of male secondary enrollment.

Equal Access to Formal Employment and Agricultural Inputs Positively Impacts Economic Growth

Gender inequalities in other dimensions besides education can also be associated with lower growth rates. Controlling for factors such as initial income, population growth, inequalities in education, and macroeconomic openness, Klasen shows that the female share of the working-age population in the formal sector has a statistically significant and positive correlation with economic growth (Klasen 1999). Where cultural norms and prejudices that discriminate against women—rather than efficiency—determine labor supply and demand in the economy, the resulting misallocation of labor means that competent female workers may be overlooked because of their sex.

A number of microeconomic studies have examined the relative productivity of men and women in farming in sub-Saharan Africa. Often, findings indicate that women farmers have lower productivity for reasons relating to poor access to resources. For example, Saito, Mekonnen, and Spurling (1994) find that the gross value of output per hectare from male-managed plots is 8 percent higher than on female-managed plots, but a study by Moock finds that if female farm managers had the same access as men to extension services and productive inputs, then their (maize) yields would be between 7 and 9 percent higher (Moock 1976). There is also evidence that the average production per farmer tends to be lower in countries in which women represent a larger share of the agricultural labor force than men do. In Sub-Saharan Africa, women are particularly disadvantaged because they often farm smaller plots of land with more uncertain tenure. In Kenya, where land title is usually a prerequisite for cooperative and producer group membership, women are often not enumerated for cash crop production. Kenyan women are also likely to be disenfranchised on widowhood or after divorce or separation (World Bank 2006c). In rural economies, reducing gender inequalities in access to agricultural inputs will therefore increase productivity. In Kenya, increasing access to agricultural inputs of female farmers to the same levels as that of male farmers could increase yields by as much as 22 percent (Quisumbing 1996). Given the importance of agriculture in Kenya's GDP, this would translate to a one-off doubling in Kenya's growth rate from 4.3 percent (in 2004) to 8.3 percent.[4]

Results from both micro- and macroeconomic regression analyses therefore conclude that gender inequality is a powerful constraint to economic growth. Applying the results from the various models suggests that if Kenya eliminated gender-based inequalities in education and access to inputs, the country could gain from a one-off increase in GDP growth by as much as 4.3 percentage points, followed by a sustained year-on-year increase in GDP growth of between 2.0 and 3.5 percentage points. Removing gender-based barriers to growth will thus make a substantial contribution to realizing Kenya's growth potential.

Notes

1. In 2005, Kenya's poverty line was defined as 1,239 (US$16.81) Kenyan shillings (K Sh) per month and as K Sh 2,648 (US$35.93) per month for rural and urban areas, respectively.

2. Sessional Paper on Gender and Development.

3. The main activities included in the household, or nonmarket, economy are subsistence production, reproductive work, and volunteer work. Subsistence production includes the production of goods for household use, such as food, clothing, furnishings, pottery, and housing. Reproductive work includes activities such as preparing meals, laundry, cleaning, and household maintenance. Voluntary work comprises unpaid activities in the community, such as self-help groups or to secure improvements in neighborhood safety.

4. In 2004, Kenya's real production of crops and horticulture was US$2.474 billion (2001 prices). Real GDP was US$14.05 billion in the same year, up from US$13.47 billion in 2003 (4.3 percent growth). A 22 percent increase in yields in 2004 would have implied crop and horticultural production of US$3.02 billion, increasing real GDP in the same year to US$14.59 billion (8.3 percent growth).

CHAPTER 3

Access to Property Rights and Land

I am totally in support of women having the right to land inheritance because I believe in gender equity and equality. Inheriting land will reduce the level of dependence of women on men, which is the basis of discrimination by the men.

—Anthony Muriithi, Volunteer, Every Child Counts (AMWIK 2006)

This chapter considers the legal framework, with a focus on women's property rights in Kenya, and applies this framework to the most important asset within the Kenyan context: land. Land is vital both because of the predominance of agriculture within the Kenyan economy and because of the significance of land in providing collateral for business finance. Yet, although women in Kenya supply 70 percent of labor in the agricultural sector, they hold only about 1 percent of registered land titles in Kenya, with around 5–6 percent of registered titles held in joint names. The chapter examines cultural and institutional reasons for women's limited land ownership and shows that women's limited ability to own land and property negatively affects their contribution to Kenya's economic growth (box 3.1). This chapter ends by making specific recommendations for reform.

Box 3.1

Attitudes to Land Run Deep

Female children should inherit land from their parents, as they are born of the same parents as the male ones. Indeed, my husband and I intend to give our daughter a share of our family land, though smaller than the one we will give to our son.

—Sarah Alex, Businesswoman

I am totally against the issue of land being inherited by women because in our Luhya tradition, land is inherited by men since the days of our forefathers. Imagine a situation where our aunties decide to come back for their share of our father's land! A constitution should be based on culture, not bringing in foreign ideas which might cause clashes within our families.

—Saul A. Anziya, Supervisor, Commission for Higher Education

Women having equal rights to inherit land will interfere with our culture, in which the natural order is that a woman comes after the man . . . . If women are allowed to inherit land, I think there will be very many cases of separation and divorce because women might use this as a weapon to rebel against men.

—Zipporah Wanjiru, Gospel Artist and Beautician

Source: AMWIK 2006.

Denial of Property Rights in Relation to Land Impacts on Poverty

The starting point for a consideration of land in Kenya is that there is not enough land available for either men or women. Only about 20 percent of the country's land is arable, with the remainder of it being classified as arid and semiarid. Seventy-five percent of Kenya's 30.4 million people live on this 20 percent. In rural areas, land is divided into about 3.5 million small farm holdings. In urban areas, a substantial proportion of the urban population has no access to land to undertake economic activity. The recent "National Land Policy Issues and Recommendations Report" pointed out that of the 10 main causes of poverty in Kenya identified in the Poverty Reduction Strategy (Government of Kenya 2005d), many had direct linkage with land issues: low productivity in crop farming and livestock farming, lack of access to land, rural unemployment, general insecurity couched in ethnic animosity, inadequate access to infrastructure and social services, and gender imbalance.

Insecure land rights can limit women from making the necessary investments in their land to increase its productivity and economic value. If claims to land are uncertain, households living at the margin are unlikely to see the value of—or feel that they can afford—investing scarce resources in soil quality, irrigation systems, or higher-value crops that require expensive inputs or offer delayed economic returns. As discussed in chapter 2, studies in different parts of the developing world have found that secure title to land is positively correlated with agricultural investments and outputs (Jacoby, Li, and Rozelle 2002; Besley 1995; Feder 1988). In Thailand, for example, a study found that gaining title to land induced higher investment in farming capital. As a result, output was 14–25 percent higher on titled land than on untitled land of equal quality (Feder 2002).

In addition, secure tenure may also contribute to the welfare of poor households by providing a form of insurance that can be used in the event of shocks or economic distress. Illness or an economic crisis can leave landless households with few resources to fall back on. In these circumstances, landowning households may be able to sell or lease out land (income smoothing) to help them through the crisis.

The Formal Legal Framework for Land Market Regulation Is Unsatisfactory, but Does Not Prevent Women from Owning Land

Kenya's legal framework regulating the land market is highly complex and fundamentally unsatisfactory. There are too many laws governing land—more than 75 in total—which, taken together, create an outdated, obscure, and highly technical regime (box 3.2). Many of these laws are obsolete; others conflict, supporting different land regimes within the same area. The problems are compounded by the poor state of land records.

Kenya's formal tenure system, introduced by the colonialists, is based on statutory registration and ownership of individually demarcated plots. But only a minority of land has been adjudicated and individual titles issued, mainly in urban areas. In other parts of the country, the land is held under various systems of group tenure (including customary law tenure and group ranching systems), or it is owned by the state (for example, government land, trust land, conservation areas, and reserves).

None of the formal laws regulating the land market prevent women from owning land. Why in practice, then, do they own so little of it?

Box 3.2

Some of Kenya's 75 Land Laws

- The Land Control Act (Cap. 302)
- Land Planning Act (Cap. 303)
- Land Acquisition Act (Cap. 295)
- Registration of Titles Act (Cap. 281)
- Land Titles Act (Cap. 282)
- Land Consolidation Act (Cap. 283)
- Land Adjudication Act (Cap. 284)
- Land (Group Representatives) Act (Cap. 287)

Women's Property Rights Are Often through a Man

Under customary law, there is a general principle that a husband should manage his wife's property, whether acquired before or during the marriage. Thus, a married woman may use matrimonial property, but she cannot dispose of it without her husband's consent.

Under customary law, the position of widows is particularly precarious. Of particular concern are the customary practices of wife inheritance and ritual cleansing, particularly (but not exclusively) among the Luo and the Luhya, which are well documented in a recent Human Rights Watch report (Human Rights Watch 2003). Wife inheritance is the long-term union of a widow and a male relative of her deceased husband, originally designed as a form of social protection and to secure her access to land. Ritual cleansing occurs by way of a short-term or one-time sexual encounter with a man paid to have sex with the widow in order to "cleanse" her from the evil spirits that are believed to contaminate her on the death of her husband. These practices take different forms in different clans, but the common thread is that a woman cannot stay in her home or have access to land unless she is inherited or cleansed. In addition to concerns that these practices exploit women's property rights and personal freedom, ritual cleansing carries with it health risks, including the risk of HIV/AIDS infection.

Because women lack control over property during their marriage, if their husbands die, it is not uncommon, particularly in rural areas, for the husbands' relatives to take the family property, including land, homes,

Box 3.3

Case Study: The Treatment of a Widow

When Susan Wagitangu's parents died, her brothers inherited the family land. "My sister and I didn't inherit," said Wagitangu, a 53-year-old Kikuyu woman. "Traditionally in my culture, once a woman gets married, she does not inherit from her father. The assumption is that once a woman gets married, she will be given land where she got married." This was not the case for Wagitangu. When her husband died, her brother-in-law forced her off that homestead and took her cows. Wagitangu now lives in a Nairobi slum.

Source: Interview with Susan Wagitangu, Nairobi, October 29, 2002 (Human Rights Watch 2003).

livestock, furniture, and household items. Many such cases are detailed in the 2003 Human Rights Watch report (box 3.3, for example).

The precise rules regarding women's property rights differ from tribe to tribe. For example, among the Maasai, Luhya, and Kisii communities, a woman may not take anything with her upon divorce. But among the Kikuyu, Damba, Tharaka, Kuria, Taita, Elgeyo Marakwet, and Tugen communities, upon divorce, a wife may take her personal effects and a share of the property if she contributed toward its acquisition (Ikdahl et al. 2005).

Formal Statute Law Gives Property Rights to Married Women

In practice, and under most customary law systems, married women in Kenya lack control over property. Formal statute law in Kenya potentially gives married women property rights. The legal situation is an emerging one and is still not entirely clear, but it does appear that the courts in Kenya are taking an increasingly liberal attitude and are now prepared to uphold women's statutory rights to property over customary laws that deny them such rights.

The Married Women's Property Act of 1882 Gives Married Women Equal Rights to Own Property

It was established in a Kenyan court in 1971[1] that the U.K. Married Women's Property Act of 1882 (MWPA) applies in Kenya as a statute of general application. The principle is thus established in Kenyan law that spouses have equal rights in ownership of property (box 3.4).

Box 3.4

The MWPA Gives Married Women Equal Rights in the Ownership of Property

- Section 1(1) provides that a married woman is capable of acquiring, holding, and disposing by will or otherwise of movable or immovable property as her separate property, in the same manner as if she were a single woman.
- Section 1(2) provides that a married woman may sue or be sued in respect of her separate property either in contract or in tort as if she were a single woman. A married woman carrying on business separately from her husband is subject to the law of bankruptcy in respect of her separate property.

It appears that the MWPA applies to all systems of marriage recognized under Kenyan law, including Muslim marriages, customary marriages, and marriages by cohabitation.[2]

The principle appears to be clear under Kenyan law: even women in customary marriages have equal property rights in the matrimonial property. However, the application of this principle in practice is less clear. Problems arise in dividing up matrimonial property on divorce or separation. If the property is in joint names, then generally it is divided equally. But what if property is in the sole name of the husband? Section 17 of the MWPA states that for a wife to successfully claim an interest in property in these circumstances, she has to show that she contributed toward the purchase of the property. This becomes particularly problematic where a woman's contribution has been nonfinancial. The Court of Appeal[3] recognized both direct and indirect financial contributions (for example, where the spouse uses her money to take care of the other aspects of the family needs, such as food and clothing) and nonfinancial contributions (for example, where a wife lives upcountry and tills the land while her husband works in an urban center and acquires property, or where the wife stays at home and takes care of the family while the husband goes to work).

The Law of Succession Act Gives Women Inheritance Rights

Under formal statute law, a woman also has very clear rights on the death of her husband to inherit his property. The Law of Succession Act of 1981[4] attempted to create a uniform law of succession for all communities of Kenya. The Succession Act governs the situation both where the deceased left a will and where he died intestate. Although it contains some discriminatory provisions, the Act does give women (and legitimate and illegitimate children) some inheritance rights on the death of their husbands (box 3.5).

The Law of Succession Act was amended in 1990 to exempt Muslims from its operations. Muslim law explicitly allows women property rights through inheritance, although their rights are not equivalent to men's (box 3.6). Yet in practice, particularly in rural areas, local customs can deny Muslim women their property rights.

Box 3.5

Law of Succession Act: Main Provisions

- If there is one surviving spouse and a child or children, the surviving spouse is entitled to—
  a. an absolute interest in the deceased personal and household effects and
  b. a life interest in the rest of the estate (that is, he or she can use them, but not dispose of them without court permission).
- If the surviving spouse is a woman, her interest in the property terminates if she remarries, but a surviving husband's interest does not terminate upon remarriage.
- When the surviving spouse dies (or in a woman's case, remarries), the estate goes to the children.
- Section 32 of the Act exempts agricultural land, crops, and livestock in certain "gazetted" districts; in these districts, customary law applies. They are West Pokot, Turkana, Samburu, Isiolo, Mandera, Wajir, Garissa, Tana River, Lamu, Kajiado, and Narok (legal notice no. 94 of 1981). Pastoral communities predominantly inhabit these districts.

Box 3.6

Muslim Inheritance Law

The *Koran's* basic intestacy rules provide that a son generally inherits double the share of a daughter. When a husband dies leaving a wife and children, the wife receives one-eighth of the net estate. If there are no children, the widow gets one-fourth of the estate. Wives in polygamous unions share the one-eighth (if there are children) or the one-fourth (if there are no children).

A Cohabiting Woman Has No Rights under Either the Formal Legal System or Customary Law

The ability of a woman to claim property rights under either the MWPA or the Law of Succession Act depends on her ability to establish her married status. There is no provision in statute law governing distribution of property for a cohabiting couple. The approach taken by the courts has been to seek to determine whether the cohabitation in fact constituted a marriage. For example, in *Mary Njoki v. John Kinyanjui and others*,[5] the appellant's claim to inherit the deceased's property was rejected, despite her cohabitation with him, because she could not prove any ceremony or ritual required for any marriage under customary law.

It Can Be Difficult to Establish Marital Status

Upon divorce, separation, or the death of a spouse, the starting point for a woman to assert her rights to property is through her marital status. This may not be easy: there are six recognized forms of marriage in Kenya.[6] Registration is not required for marriage by custom, marriage by cohabitation, and customary marriages. But in practice, the registration system is in disarray. It is scattered over several registries, which are not coordinated among themselves or with the divorce or death registries. Multiple registrations can take place under the different systems. The result is that it is often not possible to ascertain the status of an individual from inspecting a marriage register. The situation is further complicated by the fact that customary marriages and marriages by cohabitation are not registered.

The practice of polygamy further complicates the picture.[7] It is not uncommon for a woman—who thought that she was in a monogamous union—to discover on the death of her husband that there are other "wives" and children (usually married under customary law) claiming a share of the assets to which they are entitled under the provisions of the Succession Act (box 3.7).

Formal, Established Legal Principles Are Not Applied in the Vast Majority of Cases

The effect of both the MWPA and the Succession Act is to give women property rights, which case law has established override customary law. But in practice it is often extremely difficult for a woman to assert these rights. Few lawyers are fully cognizant of this complex and specialized

Box 3.7

The Succession Act Can Have the Effect of "Disinheriting" Wives

Section 3(5) of the Law of Succession Act provides that (notwithstanding the provisions of any other written law) a woman married under a system of law that permits polygamy, where her husband has contracted a previous or subsequent monogamous marriage to another woman, is nevertheless a wife for purposes of the Act. Sections 29 and 40 state that such a woman's children are accordingly children within the meaning of this Act.

area of law. Much of the law has been established through case law; however, case law in Kenya is not easily available, with official law reporting being reestablished only recently, after a break of 20 years. The result is that the law is inaccessible for advocates and judges, and the cases are not applied evenly. In matrimonial cases, the lawyer has to be aware, for example, that to secure the woman's rights the application for division of property should be made under the MWPA, rather than under the Matrimonial Causes Act[8] and the Subordinate Courts (Separation and Maintenance) Act[9]—not an obvious point.

In Practice, Many of Those Dispensing Justice—from Judges to Chiefs—Are Unaware of the Legal Position

When Human Rights Watch (Human Rights Watch 2003) discussed family property division with local officials at the community level, many had no idea that women could be entitled to anything upon separation or divorce, let alone half of the family property. One local administrator said that a woman could "not get land or property upon divorce." Judges and magistrates can make similar assumptions. The Human Rights Watch report quotes a High Court Judge as stating, "The Law of Succession Act can't apply to rural land because women are supposed to be married and go away." A magistrate is quoted as stating, "The Law of Succession Act is applied only by the educated. . . . If it is in a rural area, we don't want to interfere with the community setup."

But experience from Malawi suggests that community-based initiatives can work effectively to change local attitudes and customary norms (box 3.8).

Box 3.8

Case Study: Community Sensitization and Will-Writing Campaigns in Rural Malawi

Women's Voice, a nongovernmental organization (NGO) in Malawi, has worked to foster mass awareness of women's property and inheritance rights. Through its "will-writing" campaigns, Women's Voice sought to sensitize women and men (including traditional authorities) on women's rights, advocate for fair and equitable dispensation of property at the community level (including reform of discriminatory customary inheritance practices), and teach community members how to write a valid will and observe its provisions. The project employed the popular catchphrase, "If you don't have a will, don't die!" Women's Voice found that by collaborating with chiefs and traditional authorities, local norms concerning property and inheritance were transformed. Rather than continuing to condone property grabbing as an acceptable customary practice, chiefs have begun to refer property and inheritance cases to Women's Voice for legal advice and resolution.

Source: Strickland 2004.

Formal Registration Practices Have Excluded Women

Although only a minority of land in Kenya is formally registered with individual titles, where registration has taken place, it has clearly worked against women. As stated above, they own only about 1 percent of registered land titles in Kenya, with around 5–6 percent of registered titles held in joint names.

Various systems of land registration operate simultaneously in Kenya. The Registered Land Act (RLA)[10] commenced in 1963, with the intention of introducing a single code for the whole country. But in practice, other registration systems continue to apply alongside the RLA. For example, the Transfer of Property Act applies in formerly settler-occupied areas in the highlands, having been introduced from India during the colonial period to give settlers land rights.

The process for first registration (adjudication) of formerly unregistered land is governed by the Land Adjudication Act.[11] The Minister of Lands declares an area to be a land adjudication area. The land is consolidated into individual plots, individual land entitlements are determined, and then title is issued and registered. The new owner of the land has power to dispose of it or use it, subject only to any other interests that are noted on the title.

In practice, although under the RLA up to five people may be registered as owners of a plot of land, a plot tends to be registered in the name of just one—male—family member. Customary rights of occupation and of use are rarely noted on the register; thus, the customary rights of men are given legal force and market value. The customary rights of women are extinguished, and land ownership rights that they are given are by reference to their relationship to a man. As box 3.5 suggests, where women are given property rights, it is because of their relationship to a man.

It is fundamental to land registration systems in general, and to the RLA in particular, that the effect of registration is to grant absolute title to the registered owner of the land, subject only to interests noted on the register or rights defined as "overriding interests."[12] The legislation states that customary rights are not overriding interests unless they are registered, and the end result of a string of case law appears to be that for her user rights to be recognized, a woman must ensure that they are registered on the title. In theory, this is possible—options include registration of a caveat or an easement. But in practice, this may not be straightforward. Not only may women not be aware of their right to register their interest on the title, but the cost of doing so (including lawyers' fees) and the need to travel to an urban center to effect the registration may make the procedure impossible. Even those who succeed in effecting a registration may find that it is in practice ineffectual because of corrupt practices by land registry officials. Firm efforts clearly need to be taken by the government of Kenya to stamp out corruption in the land registries.

Allocation of State Land Has Excluded Women

A considerable proportion of land in Kenya is owned by the state, at both the national and local levels. At the national level, the Government Lands Act[13] makes provision for regulating the disposal of government land, giving the president power to alienate any such land on any terms and conditions as he thinks fit.[14] This Act has been the main avenue through which public land has been converted to individual ownership in Kenya. The FIAS Administrative Barriers Report (FIAS 2004) notes that heavily politicized and corrupt land allocation practices have meant that much government land has been transferred from state to individual ownership illegally. Because of patriarchal patronage systems in Kenya, it is highly unlikely that women have benefited significantly from this process.

At the local level, the Trust Lands Act[15] provides a framework for the administration of lands that were occupied by local Kenyans during the colonial period. These lands are now vested in local authorities, who control the development of this land. The use, disposition, and inheritance of trust land is governed by customary law. But in practice, trust land is being alienated in favor of individuals: about 40 percent of trust land is now registered with individual titles under the RLA—the vast majority with men as sole registered owners.

Family Land Can Be Disposed of without a Wife's Consent

Because women's interests are largely not noted on title deeds, the land on which they have customary user rights and on which they may depend for their livelihoods can be disposed of without their knowledge or consent. In rural areas, there may be some protection for some women through the operation of Land Control Boards (LCBs). The Land Control Act[16] controls transactions in all land that is not within a municipality, township, or market (box 3.9). Local LCBs must give consent for every transfer of land in their area, which includes its sale, lease, mortgage, or division. Appeals from the decision of an LCB go to the Provincial Land Control Appeals Board, and from there to the Central Land Appeals Board. The protection for women is based on the practice that requires family members (especially the wife) to be present as a prerequisite for consent to a transaction to be given.

Box 3.9

Factors That LCBs Must Take into Account When Determining Whether to Authorize a Land Transaction

In deciding whether to grant consent to a land transfer, section 9 of the Land Control Act provides that a Land Control Board shall (among other things)—

- have regard to the effect that the grant or refusal of consent is likely to have on the economic development of the land;
- act on the principle that consent ought generally to be refused where the person seeking to buy the land is unlikely to farm or develop the land adequately or already has sufficient land; and
- have regard to whether the terms of the transaction, including the price, are disadvantageous to one of the parties to the transaction.

From the point of view of developing Kenya's land market, the concept behind LCBs must be questioned. LCBs have a very wide discretion to decide whether to approve a particular transaction. Their processes and the appeal processes are cumbersome and time-consuming. The effects are uncertainty and additional time and cost for land transactions. Access to finance in rural areas is constrained, with banks and financial institutions prepared to accept rural land as collateral only very selectively, because the LCB system can make it difficult to realize land held as security for a loan.

The future of LCBs is not clear. The government of Kenya is currently undertaking the major process of developing a National Land Policy. The recent "National Land Policy Issues and Recommendations Report" (Government of Kenya 2005d) suggests that although institutional structures may change, the functions currently performed by the LCBs will remain. From the point of view of women, given that their interests in the land are largely not noted on the land title, the LCBs, at least in theory, provide a useful safety net. LCBs have the mandate to ensure that whenever a married man intends to dispose of rural land, he cannot do so without the consent of family members, especially his wife. In practice, however, the protection provided by LCBs in this respect is patchy at best:

- LCBs' mandate to protect family members is through an administrative directive, with no formal force of law.
- LCBs have tended to be male-dominated.
- It can be difficult to ascertain whether the wife and family members have given their consent to disposition freely.
- Anecdotally, there are many cases reported of men bringing "wives" before LCBs purportedly to give consent, while the true wife is in ignorance of the transaction.

However, a U.K. Department for International Development (DFID)–funded project is currently building LCB capacity. The capacity-building program is also for members of District Land Tribunals (DLTs), which have the function of determining disputes regarding customary land. The aim is for 30 percent of LCB members to be women and for all members to receive training, including on general issues of transparency; fairness; and the protection of women, children, and the vulnerable (box 3.10).

Box 3.10

There Is Potential for LCB Performance to Improve

Following the election in December 2002, all the then-existing members of LCBs and DLTs were removed, largely because the system that appointed them was perceived to have been corrupt. The entirely new members of the LCBs and DLTs were in urgent need of training on their role and responsibilities. The project aims to train the 7,000 members of LCBs and DLTs in Kenya's provinces and districts. The Kenya School of Law is the training agency, responsible for implementing and supervising the training program and for developing the training curriculum and training materials. The government of Kenya contributes K Sh 1.2 million to the project, as well as ongoing recurrent costs for staff, vehicles, and office space.

As of the end of August 2005, 164 LCB and LDT members had been trained. The training is being implemented in close collaboration with civil society organizations. Feedback received from the members on the training that they received has been very positive. The training materials are of a high standard and relevance, aimed at enhancing understanding of land issues, including environmental issues, HIV/AIDS, and gender. The impact of the training is assessed through regular reports that include baseline and follow-up interviews with key informants. An initial assessment suggested that there is a lack of knowledge in communities about the functions of the LCBs and DLTs.

It has been noted that, in practice, impact assessment is problematic because of difficulties in accessing some community clients, particularly widows. However, for level of knowledge of LCB and DLT members, initial indications are that the project has been particularly successful, especially regarding gender issues.

Level of Knowledge in LCB Nanyuki, Rift Valley Province

Do they have a copy of the Act, or have they read it?	1
Do they know the type of transactions they have power to deal with?	3
Do they know the procedures that must be followed?	3
Do they consider the protection of women, children, and the vulnerable in making decisions?	5
Do they know what the Act says about payment of fees to them?	3
Do they know what the Act says about payment of fees by communities?	1

1 = very weak, 5 = very good.

Source: Steyn 2005.

Women Can Be Ineligible for Cooperative Membership

Ownership of land through a title deed is a qualification for membership of most agricultural cooperatives. There are currently 9,481 cooperative societies in Kenya, and agricultural sector members make up 51 percent of total membership. The cooperatives provide important benefits to members, including mobilizing savings for lending to farmers, procurement of inputs, processing, and marketing (Ondieki et al. 2006). Only members of the cooperative are entitled to receive payment for goods sold to the cooperative. As a result, because they lack land ownership, women may be excluded from receiving payments for the outputs that their labor may have produced.

Cognizant of these issues, the Ministry of Trade and Industry commissioned a gender review of the IDA/MSME program. The review's recommendations to encourage registration of women on title deeds as members of cooperatives participating in the program were endorsed.

The Developing National Land Policy Is an Opportunity for Reform

The Minister of Lands and Housing inaugurated the National Land Policy Formulation Process in February 2004 (Government of Kenya 2004a), setting up six working groups comprising members from government, NGOs, the private sector, universities, and so forth. In August 2005, a "National Land Policy Issues and Recommendations Report" was published (Government of Kenya 2005d), setting out broad policy issues intended to provide a framework for the development of the Policy. Encouragingly, this report identifies gender as a key issue for the development of the National Land Policy (box 3.11).

These recommendations form the foundation for reform of land law that would give much greater land rights to women. But at this stage these are recommendations only. Many of them are rather broad and high-level, and some will be controversial. Further work is planned to "flesh out" these proposals and to develop widespread acceptance of them.

The Kenya Land Alliance, launched in May 1999 with funding and support from Oxfam-Kenya, is likely to play a key role in advocating for the mainstreaming of gender issues in the land policy and in developing specific reform proposals (box 3.12). The Alliance is a network of civil society organizations and individuals for effective advocacy for land law and policy reforms (Kenya Land Alliance 2002). Member organizations

Box 3.11

What the "National Land Policy Issues and Recommendations Report" Says about Gender

Culture and traditions continue to support male inheritance of family land, while there is lack of review/formulation of gender-sensitive family laws.

Recommendations

- Existing laws, regulations, customs, and practices that constitute discrimination against women in land shall be outlawed and appropriate legislation established to ensure effective protection of women against such acts.
- Succession and matrimonial property laws shall be harmonized to conform to the principle of equality between women and men.
- Review regulatory frameworks to ensure women's equal rights.
- Enact specific legislation governing division of marital property, to replace the Married Women's Property Act of 1882.
- Widows/widowers and divorcees shall be protected through the provision of co-ownership.
- Appropriate legal measures shall be taken to ensure that men and women are entitled to equal rights in land, before marriage (in cases of inheritance), during marriage, during its dissolution, and after the death of the spouse.
- Address the land markets in relation to women, especially with regard to matrimonial and family land, by enacting laws to curb selling or mortgaging family land without the involvement of both spouses.
- Define women's rights in trust/communal land.
- Promote women's access to justice in land issues and land information.

Source: Government of Kenya 2005d.

include other service organizations (for example, the Legal Assistance Centre) and networks (for example, the Shelter Forum), as well as a few community-based organizations (for example, the Ogiek Welfare Council) (Adams 2003).

Recommendations

Immediately

- Building on existing publications,[17] through the government of Kenya's GJLOS, promulgate a training manual aimed at magistrates

Box 3.12

Potential of the Kenya Land Alliance to Influence the Debate

Main objective

To mobilize individuals and institutions for effective advocacy to achieve the reform of land policy and law in Kenya

Subobjectives

- To facilitate networking and information sharing among the members and between them and others locally, regionally, and at the international level
- To sensitize and inform stakeholders and the public on the reform of land policy and law in Kenya
- To contribute to the current debate on the reform of land policy and law in Kenya
- To generate policy and legal options for land reform in Kenya
- To organize civil society groups to formulate a draft land policy for presentation to government

Source: Kenya Land Alliance 2002.

and customary leaders on women's property rights, setting out clearly case law that establishes that statute law on women's property rights prevails over discriminatory customary law.

- Monitor the impact of the training manual through considering property rights decisions at the local level (for example, market surveys undertaken by GJLOS).
- Strengthen the dissemination of knowledge about women's property rights and how women can enforce them (for example, through a radio soap, will-writing campaigns, and pamphlets such as FIDA's "ABC of Property Law").
- Prioritize publication of law reports on women's property rights through the GJLOS Reform Programme.
- Continue with training of LCB and DLT members in gender issues, and monitor impact at the local level (DFID).
- NGOs should continue to take strategic test cases to court to establish robust case law in relation to women's property rights.

In the Context of the Developing National Land Policy
- Find an appropriate way to note women's user rights on the title (for example, as an easement or as an equitable interest under a trust) and

encourage women's membership in cooperatives and access to cash remuneration through inclusion of names on land titles as part of the IDA MSME program.

- Advocate for the gender recommendations in the "National Land Policy Issues and Recommendations Report."
- Undertake institutional reform of the land registries, and ensure that corruption is eliminated.
- Monitor allocation of state land for gender bias.

In the Longer Term

- Amend the Succession Act to eliminate discriminatory provisions.
- Replace the U.K. Married Women's Property Act with a Kenyan statute, to include a presumption of spousal co-ownership of family property and equal division of family property upon separation or divorce.
- Require that all marriages be registered in the central registry, and expedite reorganization of the registry through the government's GJLOS Reform Programme.

Notes

1. In the case of *I. v. I.* (1971), *East African Law Reports* 278.
2. *Karanja v. Karanja* (1976), *Kenya Law Reports (KLR)* 307.
3. *Kivuitu v. Kivuitu* (1988–92), *Kampala Law Reports (KALR)* 2.
4. Cap. 160, Laws of Kenya.
5. Unreported Civil Appeal Case no. 71 of 1984.
6. Christian marriages under the Marriage Act or the African Christian Marriage and Divorce Act; civil marriages under the Marriage Act; Hindu marriages under the Hindu Marriage and Divorce Act; Islamic marriages under the Mohammedan Marriage and Divorce Registration Act; African customary marriages: no written law, governed by customary practices; and marriage by cohabitation.
7. Marriages conducted under the Marriage Act, the African Christian Marriage and Divorce Act, and the Hindu Marriage and Divorce Act are all monogamous. The Marriage Act makes bigamy an offense, and the Penal Code criminalizes second marriages while either spouse is still living; however, these laws do not apply to either customary or Islamic marriages, both of which are potentially polygamous. Polygamy can erode a woman's property rights.
8. Cap. 152, Laws of Kenya.
9. Cap. 153, Laws of Kenya.

10. Cap. 300, Laws of Kenya.

11. Cap. 284, Laws of Kenya.

12. Section 30 of the Act.

13. Cap. 280, Laws of Kenya.

14. Section 3.

15. Cap. 288, Laws of Kenya.

16. Cap. 302, Laws of Kenya.

17. NGOs have published excellent guides, including the Education Centre for Women in Democracy's field guide, *Succession and Inheritance in Kenya: A Handbook for Paralegals and Wananchi*. FIDA has produced an "ABC of Property Law."

CHAPTER 4

Access to Finance and Collateral

The problem here in Kenya in general is that women don't have collateral. For you to go to the bank, you must have collateral.

—Zohra Baraka, Mohazo Ex-Impo Ltd.,
Voices of Women Entrepreneurs in Kenya

Access to Affordable Finance Is a Key Constraint

Kenya has one of the most diverse financial systems in Sub-Saharan Africa, comprising 41 commercial banks, 1 development bank, 3 development finance institutions, 2 mortgage companies, 3 building societies, 2 finance companies, 43 insurance companies, and several thousand savings and credit cooperatives (SACCOs) (World Bank 2005a). Despite this, the cost and availability of finance are key constraints for many firms in Kenya, and business loans usually require collateral. The recent World Bank Investment Climate Assessment found that the cost of finance was ranked second after corruption as a major constraint to firm investment in Kenya (World Bank 2004c).

Although access to finance is an obstacle for all firms, women interviewed consistently rated it is as the single biggest constraint preventing them from growing their businesses. As already highlighted, because of

Figure 4.1. Women's Access to Resources in Kenya

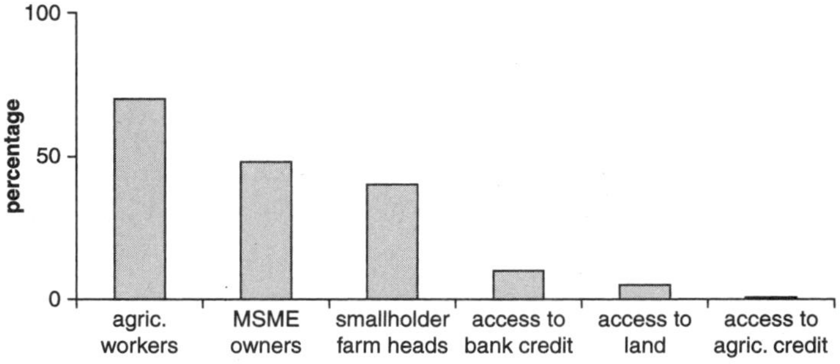

Source: Authors.

their limited land ownership, few women are able to provide the collateral needed for loan requests. Thus, even though women entrepreneurs make up nearly half of all MSME owners and 40 percent of smallholder farm managers, they have less than 10 percent of the available credit (figure 4.1) and less than 1 percent of agricultural credit (Government of Kenya 1999). The government's 2005 MSE Sessional Paper recognizes this issue: "Lack of access to credit is a major constraint inhibiting the growth of the MSME sector, and more so for women entrepreneurs" (Government of Kenya 2005e).

Informal Savings and Microfinance

Various institutions in Kenya are geared specifically toward the needs of women, such as the Kenya Women Finance Trust (KWFT), the National Association of Self-Employed Women of Kenya, and the United Women's Savings and Credit Cooperative Society (boxes 4.1 and 4.2). But these are all in the microfinance or SACCO sectors. Informal enterprises are served by more than 5,000 microfinance institutions (MFIs) and SACCOs, the latter being the biggest provider of microfinance to MSMEs in the country (Coetzee, Kabbucho, and Minjama 2002).

However, the microfinance sector is highly segmented and disconnected. MFIs target different market niches and operate under different methodologies and organizational missions. The majority of Kenyan MFIs, especially the nonbank ones, often lack the financial and institutional capacity to diversify their lending products and offer business support programs to their clients. Larger and formalized enterprises may have access to commercial

Box 4.1

Kenya Women Finance Trust

Started in 1981 and the first African affiliate of Women's World Banking, KWFT is today the largest provider of microfinance in Kenya targeting women. The organization had 78,786 active members at the end of 2005 and more than 300 staff servicing low-income women. KWFT has wide reach in seven of Kenya's eight provinces, and it provides both group-based and individual loans. The average loan size is K Sh 36,125, and the self-sufficiency rate is 119 percent.

Source: www.kwft.org.

Box 4.2

United Women's Savings and Credit Cooperative Society (UWSACCO)

Created in 2000 by a team of professional women, UWSACCO's mission is to help women acquire financial assets that will give them economic power and financial freedom. Their vision is to transform UWSACCO into a women's savings bank. UWSACCO targets the upper end of women MSME business owners and NGO women executives with higher savings requirements (K Sh 100,000 minimum savings) and bigger loans (average of K Sh 250,000). Prospective members are interviewed and closely screened before being granted membership status. Most prospective members are introduced by current members. The committee prefers this approach because it transfers some of the screening requirements to the sponsoring members.

The success of the UWSACCO is well captured in its financial statements. As of May 2005, the share capital grew from K Sh 6,954,045 to K Sh 16,460,269, reflecting a growth of 137 percent. Total loans grew from K Sh 4.5 million to K Sh 10.5 million, reflecting a growth of 33 percent. As of November 2005, the default rate was zero. But UWSACCO's membership is small and exclusive. In interviews, UWSACCO's leadership indicated they believe that the lack of legal and regulatory framework governing the operations of the SACCOs is the biggest threat to the organization.

banks and licensed nonbank financial institutions. There is virtually no provision between these two extremes.

Even though well-delivered microfinance is a great poverty reduction tool, it offers only limited support for women who wish to grow their enterprises beyond the micro level. Women business owners who have outgrown the maximum loan limits from microfinance institutions have great difficulties obtaining loans as small as K Sh 1 million from commercial banks.

The "Missing Middle" in Financial Services

Commercial banks provide the widest range of services, but until recently, they were not interested in servicing Small and Medium Enterprises (SMEs) because of the perception of the higher credit risk and the high transaction costs. With an improved macroeconomic framework and lower interest rates, more banks are recognizing the potential of lending to SMEs and are developing products to target this growing sector. For example, Equity Bank provides financial literacy training and same-day emergency loans for MSMEs. Its product range and marketing strategy directly target women entrepreneurs.

The lack of data (including sex-disaggregated data) on the current SME sector and the lack of "lending know-how" affect the availability and cost of banks' financial products for SMEs.[1] It is encouraging that Standard Chartered Bank is currently undertaking a study on the SME sector to better understand the segmentation of its customer base, including by gender, and is developing its SME lending strategy.

Despite some positive trends by the banks in reaching out to the MSMEs, women entrepreneurs report that they continue to encounter gender bias when they approach a traditional financial institution. Discriminatory treatment by bank officials who prefer dealing with husbands and often do not take women seriously is a frequently cited issue (box 4.3).

In response to women entrepreneurs' need for financing and formal training, two major initiatives by international agencies have been launched in 2006. The African Development Bank's (AfDB's) Growth-Oriented Women Entrepreneurs (GOWEs) program provides US$10 million to four banks, with a 50 percent guarantee, for on-lending to women entrepreneurs. The accompanying US$2 million technical assistance component to train bank credit staff to provide nondiscriminatory service and to up-skill women entrepreneurs in business and financial management skills is managed by the IFC. In addition, as part of the

Box 4.3

Women Can Face Discrimination When Approaching a Bank for Financing

Diana Mulili is the codirector of Inform Creative Interiors, a company that has been providing interior design and architecture services in the East African region since 1998. The company's clients include ActionAid International, PTA bank, and African Trade Insurance. Access to finance has been a major issue for Inform Creative Interiors. "We have had challenges in terms of financing. They are always demanding collateral," Diana says. "That's our biggest problem." Dealing with the banks has proved particularly challenging for her as a woman. "The bank always prefers to deal with the husband," she says. "They feel that maybe I am not the key decision maker." To address the issue of financing, the company is setting up systems and structures to attract other shareholders and eventually venture capitalists.

Source: Cutura 2006.

World Bank Group IDA MSME program, the IFC SME Solutions Center in Nairobi is providing technical assistance to complement more than US$10 million in debt and equity funds managed by the South African-based firm Business Partners. The program is targeting one-third women.

The Legal and Regulatory Framework for SME Finance Is Incomplete

MFIs are governed by separate legal frameworks and administered by different government agencies. Bank MFIs are regulated and supervised by the Central Bank of Kenya (CBK), and SACCOs are regulated and supervised by the Cooperative Ministry. Financial service associations are not regulated or supervised by any government entity.

The government has drafted a Microfinance Bill to provide the legal framework for supervised MFIs' operations, but the bill has not yet passed cabinet approval. The bill is a good step toward better CBK supervision of the MFI sector, but amending the Banking Bill and building the capacity of the Central Bank should be a higher priority.

A SACCO bill has also been drafted to provide the legal and regulatory framework necessary for the supervision of SACCOs, but the bill has not yet been passed by Parliament. There are serious concerns about the financial viability of several SACCOs: a study conducted by the World Council of Credit Unions demonstrated a high loan delinquency and significant undercapitalization (Wanjau and Ndolo 2003). The need to address the issue is pressing, because the failure of even a small SACCO will have a tremendous effect on the financial infrastructure in Kenya and will shake consumer confidence in nonbank MFIs. In November 2005, the Akiba microfinance institution was closed by the Central Bank for illegally collecting deposits. The publicity surrounding the event should pressure the Ministry of Finance to quicken the enactment process.

Women Entrepreneurs Are Not Rewarded for Their Repayment History

Women entrepreneurs' main asset is their credit history because women's repayment rates (especially in microfinance) are often higher than men's, but the lack of a credit-referencing system means that valuable MFI information on SME businesses is not available to other financial institutions nor within the financial system generally.[2] The key impact of the limited availability of credit information is that collateral requirements in Kenya are high, and overcollateralization practice is common. The 2004 Investment Climate Survey found that 86 percent of loans required collateral and that the average value of the collateral was nearly twice that of the loan. In the vast majority of cases, the collateral required is land—usually land that has registered title.

The frequent requirement for land as collateral means that many women are unable to take the step up from MFIs and SACCOs to formal collateral-based lending. But women often own assets that they could potentially use as collateral. These are in the form of "movable" property (for example, stock, machinery, and book debts). In practice, these types of assets are infrequently used as security for a loan, except in the context of a fixed and floating charge taken over all of the assets of a limited liability company.

Lending institutions in Kenya face huge problems in assessing and managing risk. Even basic creditworthiness information is difficult to obtain, what with the Companies Registry in disarray and no enforcement of the requirement to file annual returns. Delays and inefficiencies in the courts make it difficult to take action against bad debtors. Kenya does not have a credit bureau that could capture women's excellent repayment histories at the micro level, enabling them to present their successful business track records to formal financial institutions in lieu of collateral.

The limited availability of basic credit information and the lack of a system for banks to share what information they have impacts even more on women entrepreneurs, whose main asset is their credit history. Recent efforts (led by the IFC, in cooperation with the Central Bank and the Ministry of Finance) to address this issue and establish a credit reference bureau are encouraging and should disproportionately benefit women.

Law Reform Could Enable Nonland Assets to Be Used as Collateral

How can the value of these assets, frequently the only ones available to women, be realized as a means of accessing finance? Part of the answer may lie in law reform. Kenya's current framework regulating the creation, ranking, and realization of nonland-secured interests is unworkable (box 4.4).

The "Barriers to Investment" report (FIAS 2004) recommends that Kenya's movable property law should undergo fundamental reform and that Kenya should adopt a new code for the regulation of nonland securities. The report specifically recommends the adoption of a regime that has been successfully used in many common law jurisdictions for many years and is universally regarded as an international best practice. This is a regime based on article 9 of the United States Uniform Commercial Code. The report notes that such a reform would result in Kenya having for the first time a comprehensive system for recognizing and ranking security interests in personal property, replacing existing registers and regimes (including the current part IV of the Companies Act,[3] relating to the registration of charges). This would radically simplify the theory and practice of the law and thereby reduce the complexity of transactions. It would enable floating charges—a highly useful and flexible instrument for secured lending—to be available to all businesses, not just those large and formal enough to be registered under the Companies Act. Evidence from the World Bank's *Doing Business in 2006* report suggests that undertaking this type of reform works (box 4.5).

Such a reform would benefit all businesses. But it would be of particular benefit to women, with so little land to use as collateral, potentially enabling them to unleash the value of their assets to generate finance for their businesses. Encouragingly, the World Bank/DFID-funded Financial and Legal Sector Technical Assistance Project includes reforms in this area.

The government of Kenya, with donor support, is undertaking numerous initiatives to address the major weaknesses of the financial system

Box 4.4

The Legal Framework for Using Nonland Assets as Collateral Is Not in Place

Kenya's current legal framework regulating movable property securities has a number of serious problems:

- **It is scattered.** Kenya does not have a uniform code for the regulation of secured interests in movable property. There is no comprehensive framework for recognizing and ranking security interests. The current law can be found in part IV of the Companies Act,[a] which regulates charges over the assets of a registered company; the Chattels Transfer Act, which regulates security given by an individual or a partnership; the Hire Purchase Act, which regulates hire purchase agreements; and common law, which addresses particular types of security interests such as retention of title clauses.
- **It is inconsistent.** The legal requirements associated with different types of security interests (for example, registration) are not consistent. They depend on both the nature of the debtor (whether or not it is a company) and the nature of the agreement (for example, the Companies Act and the Chattels Transfer Act require registration, but other arrangements—such as retention of title clauses—do not).
- **It is technical.** Some of the requirements are extremely rigid (for example, the provision that charges against the assets of a company are void unless they are registered within a strict time limit).
- **It is incomplete.** There is need for priority certainty and other matters without recourse to common law (for example, the powers and duties of receivers are currently not codified).
- **It is unfair.** Unfairness can occur to both debtors and innocent purchasers of personal property. For example, there are circumstances in which an innocent purchaser can be deprived of title to the property that he or she has purchased because of a security interest of which the purchaser was unaware and of which he or she was unable to have become aware.[b]

Source: FIAS 2004.

a. Broadly, the Act provides that any charge over the assets of a company must be registered in the Companies Registry within 42 days of creation, or it is potentially void. Registration in the Companies Registry fixes all persons with constructive notice of the charge.

b. This is the result of the operation of the common law rule *nemo dat quod non habet* (no one can give what one does not have). An innocent purchaser cannot receive a better title to property than the seller had. For example, if title to the property is in fact held by a lender (for example, under a retention of title clause or hire purchase agreement), the seller does not have a title to pass on to the purchaser.

Box 4.5

Law Reform on Using Nonland Assets as Collateral Has Worked Well Internationally

In 1999, Romania undertook a package of measures—including law reform to make it easier for a wider range of nonland assets to be used as collateral, with a clear legal framework. Since then, more than 200,000 notices of security interest were registered. The number of borrowers increased threefold, and the volume of credit by 50 percent. Following similar reform in the Slovak Republic, more than 70 percent of new business credit was secured by nonland-secured transactions.
Source: World Bank 2006a.

and is committed to reforms to improve the enabling environment for financial sector development. These initiatives include the development of a comprehensive sector strategy to streamline and clarify the legal and regulatory framework governing different classes of financial institutions and to promote linkages between financial institutions (FIs), the strengthening of debt markets, the restructuring of state-owned financial institutions, the improvement of the legal and regulatory framework for MFIs' operations, the improvement of the lending environment, the reform of the commercial justice system, and the elimination of corruption. These initiatives are supported by the following programs:

- The Financial and Legal Sector Technical Assistance Project (FLSTAP), funded by the World Bank and DFID
- The Financial Sector Deepening Trust (FSDT), a former DFID initiative, now part of the MSME Competitiveness project, an IDA/IFC project
- The recently approved Kenya Financial Sector Adjustment IDA Credit (FSAC)

Recommendations

Immediately
- Advance the reform of part IV of the Companies Act, the Chattels Transfer Act, and common law in relation to movable property securities law by enacting a best-practice regime based on article 9 of the U.S.

Uniform Commercial Code, as adapted for use in common law countries (for example, New Zealand). Prioritize for immediate action under FLSTAP.

- Collect and report sex-disaggregated data on the MSME sector by ensuring that future surveys and mapping exercises are gender-sensitive, and ensure that, in addition to the number of employees, the minimum financial need criteria are used to better profile MSMEs.
- Collect and strengthen legislation to enable efficient exchange of credit information between financial institutions, especially between MFIs and banks, leading to comprehensive coverage through a credit reference bureau.
- Encourage provision of financing mechanisms for female-owned businesses through local financial institutions and international development institutions.

Notes

1. Conversations with a Standard Chartered Bank representative.
2. During the March 2, 2006, East Africa Credit Reporting Conference, in Nairobi, Kenya, participants highlighted the importance of credit reporting in facilitating more financing to SMEs, because credit information is used to improve portfolio risk management. The governor of the Central Bank, Dr. Andrew Mullei, estimated that the growth of credit reporting would, therefore, benefit about 1.3 million micro and small enterprises in Kenya that employ an estimated 2.4 million people and contribute approximately 18.4 percent of Kenya's GDP. The government estimates the SME sector to have grown at 11 percent annually (from 1.3 million in 1999).
3. Cap. 488, Laws of Kenya.

CHAPTER 5

Access to the Formal Sector: Business Entry and Licensing

Business registration is very cumbersome. If you are a woman, you do not have time.

—Mary Okello, Makini Schools, *Voices of Women Entrepreneurs in Kenya*

The Government of Kenya Recognizes the Importance of the MSME Sector to Employment Creation and Economic Growth

Kenya's informal economy is vibrant and growing. Total employment in the informal sector is estimated to have reached more than 5 million by 2002 (an increase from 3.7 million in 1999). The formal sector saw hardly any increase from its 1.74 million employees over the same period (Government of Kenya 2003b). The *Economic Recovery Strategy for Wealth and Employment Creation 2003–2007 (ERS)* estimated that only 12 percent of the 2,636,130 jobs expected to be created over the 2003–07 period would be in the formal sector. The government of Kenya is committed to growing the MSME sector, noting in the *ERS* that the "policy focus during the recovery period will be increasingly on the small business enterprises" (Government of Kenya 2003b).

Yet Many Women Are "Stuck" Running Micro Enterprises in the Informal Sector

Most Kenyan enterprises that operate informally are micro or small. More than 99 percent of MSMEs employ fewer than 10 people, and many employ much fewer than 10.[1] Yet the 1999 National Micro and Small Enterprise Survey highlighted the growing contribution that MSMEs are making to Kenya's economy. Their contribution to GDP increased from 14 percent in 1993 to more than 18 percent in 1999. The fact that female-owned firms tend to be small, as noted in chapter 2, is the source of many of their problems. Global evidence suggests that the smaller the firm, the greater the obstacles it faces—in relation to financing, taxes, regulation, inflation, corruption, street crime, and anticompetitive practices.

Registration Is an Important Step for Business Growth

Most MSMEs are not registered. As of 1999, under 12 percent of them had undertaken the registration process, and less than 40 percent of them operated with any form of business license (Government of Kenya 1999). How can Kenyan women be enabled to grow their businesses? There is evidence that formalization of their businesses through registration is a key step. Kenyan firms that are registered are significantly more likely to grow than those that are unregistered:

> *Registration seems to be an epoch in the lifecycle of informal firms and is crucial for firm graduation. This finding leads to the conclusion that informality imposes major penalties on firms with uncertain legal status that reduces access to credit and public services such as electricity, telephone and water, all of which are important for improved performance and graduation.* (ACEG 2003)

Women May Respond Well to Simplified Registration Procedures

Why do so few women MSME owners register their businesses, and how can registration rates be improved? Women tend to be "time-poor," combining family duties with running their businesses, and they have limited access to financial resources. The time and cost involved in the registration process may literally make registration impossible for many women. And the time and cost involved are considerable. Research commissioned by the Deregulation Project of the Kenya Institute of Public Policy Research and Analysis suggests that the management time and cost involved in undertaking the registration of business names and securing of trade licenses (two basic forms of registration and licensing applicable to small businesses) together cost Kenya about 1 percent of GDP each year (KIPPRA 2000). A 2004 Regulatory Cost Survey in Uganda found that trade license procedures have a particularly negative impact on women. Although the procedures were an obstacle for a little more than 30 percent of men, 40 percent of women cited this as an obstacle to their business growth (Kirkpatrick and Lawson 2004). For women with access to financial resources who can afford a lawyer to handle the procedures, the burden may not be so great (box 5.1), but for most women in Kenya, this is not an option.

A recent World Bank Urban Informal Sector Investment Climate Analysis in Kenya, which surveyed 250 firms in Nairobi and its environs, revealed that, on average, women perceive tax rates, tax administration, and customs to be greater constraints to business growth than men do (figure 5.1). Taxes and customs are costs of formalization, and this negative perception thus decreases the likelihood that women will register their businesses.

One possible explanation for this difference in perception is that government officials are enforcing regulations differently for women. As the World Bank survey notes, taxes and customs constraints are areas that require greater interactions with government officials. Interviews with women entrepreneurs reveal that negative attitudes and intimidation

Box 5.1

Registration and Licensing Are Time-Consuming, Expensive, and Unpleasant

A director of a restaurant in Nairobi stated that to register her business as a company, she sought professional advice. "We involved a lawyer who handled the process, so that was not difficult." Yet securing necessary business licenses was a different issue. "Being in the restaurant business, there are all these regulations and all these licenses we have to get. There are too many licenses, and they cost so much money." Being a female business owner made the process only more difficult for Roseanne. "They tend to harass a woman. I've had an incident. It was men who came to inspect. I told my chef to handle the matter with them. When they deal with another man, there is only so much they will push. But with a woman, they push you to the wall."

Source: Cutura (2006).

Figure 5.1. Women Perceive Tax and Customs as a Greater Constraint to Business Growth

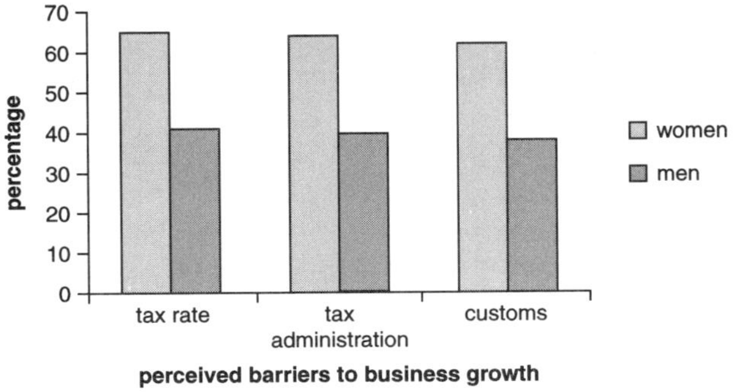

perceived barriers to business growth

Source: World Bank 2006b.

by government officials are a major issue in their interactions with civil servants. Ensuring that women are not treated unfairly in their interactions with the government will thus be an important step to encourage women to formalize their businesses and help achieve the government of Kenya's economic growth targets.

There is evidence that women may respond well to a simplification of registration and licensing procedures. Neighboring Uganda has almost identical registration and trade licensing requirements to Kenya's. A recent pilot project undertaken by the Ministry of Finance, Planning, and Economic Development's Regulatory Best Practice Programme suggests that when registration/licensing requirements are simplified, more women come into compliance and formalize their enterprises (box 5.2).

Registration of Business Names Act: Fundamental Reform Required

There are two forms of business registration in Kenya, in addition to the complex business-licensing regime discussed later in this chapter. Businesses can be registered under either the Registration of Business Names Act[2] or the Companies Act.[3] Business names registration is the more straightforward of the two processes. Firms that are not registered as companies are required to undertake business name registration if they are operating under a name that is not the surname of the owner or the surnames of the partners. The process of business names registration is described in box 5.3.

Box 5.2

Reducing Compliance Costs Increases Compliance—Especially among Women

The Regulatory Best Practice Programme in Uganda has started pilot projects to reduce the time and monetary cost of obtaining trade licenses by streamlining licensing procedures and reducing the number of approvals. The Impact Assessment on the first pilot at Entebbe (which has recently won an International Investors award) suggests that the reforms were encouraging female-owned enterprises to obtain licenses for the first time. Most of the license applications from women were first-time registrations. The second pilot at Mukono is in its initial stages. Initial information from it suggests that while female-owned enterprises wanted to formalize and began the license application procedure, there was a high dropout rate—because they were deterred by the complex system and gave up.

Source: UMACIS 2000.

The FIAS Kenya Administrative Barriers Report argues persuasively that the current business names registration regime is fundamentally flawed and unduly onerous and imposes costs that far outweigh its benefits. It points out that other common law jurisdictions have demonstrated that a much lighter and more focused regulatory regime is a satisfactory way to address the mischief that the Registration of Business Names Act was enacted to prevent. Unincorporated firms that wish to protect their business names have alternative mechanisms through which to do so: by registration of a business name under the Trade Marks Act and by way of common law "passing off" actions. In any event, the current system in Kenya is not enforced in practice and therefore totally fails in its purpose.

The FIAS report contains the strong recommendation that the business names registration regime should be fundamentally reformed in line with international best practices. A key element of the reform should be to review the Registration of Business Names Act so as to have a streamlined regime that complies with international best practices (for example, the U.K. Business Names Act of 1985).

It is of concern that current initiatives in Kenya aimed at simplifying registration and licensing procedures do not take this best-practice

Box 5.3

Business Names Registration Is Time-Consuming and Costly

To register a business name under the Registration of Business Names Act requires a search of the Business Names Registry (cost: K Sh 200), and if the search reveals that the business name has not been claimed, the name can then be registered (cost: K Sh 800).

It is not possible to search and register by mail; searches and registrations must be performed in person at the Registrar General's Department in Nairobi. It usually takes two or three days to search the Business Names Registry, although it can, occasionally, take up to a month. The Registry contains approximately 400,000 business names, and in 2003, nearly 20,000 businesses were registered.[a] Although the registration fee is relatively modest, the requirement to personally attend to the process, which can take several days, means that the process is cumbersome, bureaucratic, and costly, especially for small businesses. It is even more likely to be a burden for women, with their multiple responsibilities.

Many unincorporated businesses operate without registering their business names. Although the Act prescribes a penalty of a three-month imprisonment or a fine[b] for trading without registration, in practice, the Registrar General's Department does not enforce these provisions. Instead, enforcement usually occurs when a business seeks financing through a financial institution or when a local authority or the Kenya Revenue Authority (particularly when a business seeks to formalize its operations) notices that the business has not been registered. The authorities then insist that registration must occur. This insistence by financial institutions that a business formally register its name imposes a barrier to credit, particularly for small and informal businesses in Kenya, and especially those outside Nairobi.

A business that ceases trading must deregister its business name, but in practice, deregistration rarely occurs. One suspects that a significant proportion of the 400,000 registered names are in fact associated with defunct businesses.

Source: FIAS 2004.
a. Registrar General's Department.
b. Sections 10 and 25.

approach, but instead are intending to retain a streamlined version of the current registration system (box 5.4). It is recommended that the approach taken to business names registration under these ongoing initiatives be urgently reviewed in light of international best practices.

Box 5.4

Current Business Name Registration Reform Could Do More

The World Bank–funded MSME Project (under its Improving the Business Environment component) aims to reduce the costs of business start-ups through introducing one-stop shops. The aim is for businesses to be able to finalize all registration and licensing requirements—including business permits, tax identification numbers, trade licenses, and business name registration—at one center.

The Working Committee on Regulatory Reforms for Business Activity in Kenya is currently spearheading a "guillotine process" aimed at deregulating Kenya's complex registration and licensing regime. But the approach taken to business name registration is to simplify procedures, rather than abolishing the registration system altogether.

Companies Act Registration: Best-Practice Business Entry Reform Required

Unlike registration under the Registration of Business Names Act, registration under the Companies Act has the effect of "incorporating" the business, giving it its own legal identity and giving its owners the incentive to take risks through the protection afforded by limited liability status. For many small businesses, however, these benefits may not be clear; as a result, the majority of businesses are registered under the Registration of Business Names Act. By international standards, incorporation is lengthy and cumbersome (box 5.5).

The FIAS report recommends a fundamental simplification of this process, in line with international best practices in similar jurisdictions. Box 5.6 presents a summary of the FIAS recommendations in this respect. This study endorses these recommendations.

Companies Act Registration Facilitates the Pooling of Resources

Company registration is currently much more complex and expensive than business name registration, largely because of the requirement to use an advocate (lawyer) to draw up company documents for filing. But if Kenya were to reform its Companies Act in line with (say) the New Zealand Act (which is generally regarded as best Commonwealth practice), then Companies Act registration would involve a do-it-yourself filling in of a single form, with no requirement for lengthy legal documents as at present.

Box 5.5

Outdated and Cumbersome Procedures to Incorporate a Company

The procedure for registration is set out in the Companies Act,[a] which is modeled on the 1948 Companies Act of England and Wales. Registration is effected by filing documents at the Registrar General's Department in Nairobi. Although the registry accepts postal applications, 98 percent of applicants apply in person or use a surrogate agent[b] to follow up on the registration process. The Registrar General's Department reports that the average time for registration is two weeks, although the private sector perception is that the process can take much longer. Kenya has more than 100,000 registered companies, and 6,000 new registrations occurred in 2003.

Registration occurs in two stages. The first step involves registering a company name, which occurs by completing a form stating the desired name of the company and paying a fee of K Sh 15,000, which reserves the proposed name for 30 days. The second step of the process is to file the following documents with the Registrar General:

• Memorandum
• Articles of association
• Information regarding directors and secretary
• Statement of nominal capital
• Notice of registered office
• Declaration of compliance sworn before a Commissioner for Oaths

Following the issuing of a new amendment in 2006, lawyer fees are no longer charged on a sliding scale. The amendment states that for the formation and incorporation of companies with share capital, the advocate will charge such fees as may be agreed between the advocate and the client, but not less than Kshs.50,000. In practice, the minimum fee is likely to be considered too high by many Kenyans.

Source: FIAS 2004.
a. Cap. 486, Laws of Kenya.
b. Registrar General's Department.

Box 5.6

Companies Act Reform: Recommendations on Entry Procedures

The current system of registering a company in Kenya is bureaucratic, technical, and lengthy. It is therefore not surprising that business entry procedures (including registration) cost more than 50 percent of gross national income per capita—compared with only 1 percent in the United Kingdom, for example. Despite the benefits of limited liability status, most formal businesses in Kenya choose to register via the Registration of Business Names Act, rather than the Companies Act (in 2003, the former had 20,000 business name registrations, whereas the latter had 6,000 company registrations).

Kenya is therefore urged to amend its Companies Act to simplify registration procedures by—

- abolishing the requirement to reserve a name before registration,[a]
- abolishing the requirement to file memorandums and articles of association,
- establishing a straightforward application form for registration, and
- amending its Advocates Act to remove advocates' monopoly on preparing company formation documents.

Best-practice models for reform are Australia, Canada, and New Zealand (but not England and Wales, where best-practice reform has not taken place, largely because of the impact of European Community requirements).

Source: FIAS 2004.
a. Section 19 of the Companies Act does not specify name reservation as a requirement, although it is treated as such in practice.

One of the major advantages of company as a business form is that share structure is an effective mechanism to facilitate the pooling of resources, enabling business growth. As described above, many women in Kenya operate their businesses alone, perhaps with the support of family members. Joint enterprises appear to be rare. But this is not the experience as far as women's groups at the community level are concerned. Women in Kenya frequently join community groups to pool their resources and undertake joint activities, which range from providing communal agricultural labor to food processing and even running transport firms. It is estimated that there are more than 120,000 such groups in Kenya, encompassing 4.7 million women and umbrella groups that can command large resources. Concerns have been expressed about the politicization of some of these groups and also about their lack of accountability in financial affairs, particularly in the context of *harambee* ("pulling together" in Swahili, a Kenyan tradition of community self-help events, such as fund-raising) (Transparency International-Kenya 2003).

But the fact remains that women in Kenya appear, at least at the community level, to perceive benefits in pooling resources and in undertaking joint initiatives. However, the legal model that they are using to do so is far from ideal: there is insufficient regulatory control and protection for members, management structures can be cumbersome, and they do not have the benefit of limited liability status. A reformed Companies Act with simplified procedures has the potential to provide an alternative vehicle to enable women to take such initiatives forward within a more formal business context.

Business Licensing Requirements Are Onerous

Multiple licenses are required for nearly all business activities in Kenya, with overlapping central and local government requirements. Although licenses often are necessary to ensure compliance with regulatory requirements, they can entail excessive time and cost obligations and are also an entry point for corrupt practices and harassment. The recent World Bank Investment Climate Assessment found that corruption was rated as a severe or major obstacle by 74 percent of the sample of businesses interviewed, much more than neighboring countries.[4] More than half the firms interviewed reported having to make unofficial payments worth more than 6 percent of revenues. Some of the worst offenders included the taxation authority and municipal authorities.

Although unnecessary and burdensome licenses impose time and costs on all businesses in Kenya, it is likely that their impact is more severe on women than on men. Not only are women who are time and financially poor more constrained than men in obtaining the licenses, but they are more likely to be subjected to demands for unauthorized payments and harassment. The evidence from Uganda, which has a similar licensing regime to Kenya, is that once licensing procedures are simplified, female-owned businesses respond well and come into compliance (box 5.3).

An Ambitious and Badly Required Overhaul of All Business Licenses

In 2005, the government launched a review of all business licenses in Kenya. The reform applies a simple fast-track review process to find out what licenses can be eliminated, simplified, or maintained. Unless regulators can justify that licenses are legal, necessary, and business-friendly, the licenses are eliminated by default or recommended for simplification. This "guillotine approach" reverses the burden of proof, because defenders of the status quo must prove that current licensing practices are justified. The review has identified some 1,300 licenses, including more than 400 local authority licenses, for elimination or simplification.

The license reform does not stop with review and elimination of existing licenses. It also includes parallel efforts to build institutional capacities to prevent reemergence of poor licensing practices. First, an Electronic Regulatory Registry will be set up to host all valid business licenses, and the principle will be that a license has to be listed in the Registry to be legally binding. The Registry will work as an information center for businesses and the general public and will permit investors to identify the licenses required and to download application forms and supporting information. Second, a Regulatory Quality Review Unit will be set up to "guard the gates" to the Registry. The Unit will be responsible for screening all new licenses before they become legal and are accepted into the Regulatory Registry. The Unit, to be located within the Ministry of Finance, will ensure that all future laws and regulations related to the business and investment environment meet a simple "quality test"—a regulatory impact assessment—before enactment. This Unit will also develop and implement a medium-term regulatory reform strategy and monitor the quality of new licenses.

Current Business Licensing Reforms Should Have a Gender Lens

The Committee did not specifically examine whether particular licenses disproportionately impact on women. The focus was on a comprehensive review of all business licenses on the basis of their legality, efficiency, and relevance.

It will be essential to ensure that this important reform initiative effectively addresses licensing requirements in those sectors of the economy that predominantly involve women. Survey evidence indicates the clustering of women in particular sectors. For example, the 1999 MSME Baseline Survey pointed to the fact that 75 percent of MSMEs in the trade sector were owned by women. The recent World Bank MSME Investment Climate Survey found that women predominated in food processing, beer brewing, hairdressing, dressmaking, and retail of secondhand clothing, whereas male-owned enterprises were focused around metal work, carpentry, vehicle repair, shoemaking, construction, and transport.

Results So Far Are Promising, but More Is Needed

The license reform in Kenya is well under way, but far from over. To date, the Kenyan government has committed itself to eliminating 118 licenses and to simplifying another 700 licenses. Additional license eliminations are likely to follow as the review process continues throughout 2006, including review of licenses issued by local governments. Full implementation of the reform is pending parliamentary approval of a Business Regulation Reform Bill.

Recommendations

Immediately

- Expedite the review of the overall steps for business registration, which is taking place under the World Bank IDA MSME Competitiveness project, with a view to simplifying the steps and associated costs, and develop a one-stop shop for business registration, business name registration, and other regulations.
- Expedite the process of replacing the Companies Act with a new regime based on international best practices in common law countries (for example, Australia, Canada, and New Zealand), in particular to streamline business entry procedures.

- The government must follow through on the steps and commitments already taken to implement the Business License Reform. In particular, the government must
  - assure that the required legal measures are submitted in a timely fashion to Parliament and receive legislative priority on the parliamentary agenda;
  - maintain a centralized and stringent application of the guillotine approach for the remaining 700 national government licenses and for all local government licenses; and
  - establish the Regulatory Review Unit and the Electronic Regulatory Registry, and ensure that appropriate mechanisms are in place to screen *new* business licenses and, at a later stage, other business regulation.

Notes

1. Small firms are defined as those with 10–49 employees. Micro firms have 1–9 employees. They are defined as not including farm holdings, except farm-based enterprises that involve processing (Government of Kenya 1999).

2. Cap. 499, Laws of Kenya.

3. Cap. 486, Laws of Kenya.

4. ICS 2002/03 survey of more than 280 formal manufacturing firms and workers in seven subsectors in Nairobi, Mombasa, Eldoret, Kisumu, and Nakuru.

CHAPTER 6

Access to Justice

*[My business] has been locked up in many court battles. That in itself makes
growing a business difficult.*

—Esther Passaris, Adopt A Light, *Voices of Women Entrepreneurs in Kenya*

Limited Access to Formal Courts; Limited Justice in Informal Courts

In addition to property rights, having access to justice is vital for business
operations—for enforcing contracts, for employment disputes, and to
provide a sound foundation for collateral-based lending. Yet women in
Kenya face particular obstacles when accessing justice. When seeking to
enforce their rights, women in Kenya need to access a variety of courts.
Take the example of the division of matrimonial property: issues arising
from civil and Christian marriages are dealt with by the High Court and
the Magistrates Court; the Kadhis (Islamic) Court and the High Court
have jurisdiction to deal with these issues in relation to Islamic marriages;
and the District Magistrates Court has jurisdiction to deal with issues
arising from customary marriages.

But formal courts in Kenya are generally too costly, time-consuming,
complex, and geographically inaccessible for many Kenyans, particularly

those in rural areas. Enforcing a contract in Kenya is costly not only by international standards but even in comparison with doing so in neighboring Uganda and Tanzania (table 6.1).

Even in the formal courts, negative attitudes toward women can still prevail (box 6.1).

According to FIDA, a woman can generally obtain justice in relation to issues such as property rights if she can get her case heard in the High Court, where principles applied will be generally in line with statute law and decided case law. Outside of the High Court, FIDA's experience is that it is more difficult for a woman to obtain justice. It is not unusual for magistrates to overlook and misinterpret family property and succession laws. But in practice, the only justice available for many Kenyans is that dispensed by local chiefs or elders. For women, this presents particular problems. Even if a woman is aware of her rights, she may in practice be unable to enforce them. Chiefs and councils of elders nearly always comprise only male members, and the justice they dispense is customary justice, which, although accessible and cheap, perpetuates male dominance in issues such as inheritance and property rights (box 6.2).

Table 6.1. Cost of Enforcing a Contract in Selected Commonwealth Countries

Country	Time (days)	Cost (percentage of debt)
New Zealand	**50**	4.8
Botswana	**154**	24.8
Uganda	**209**	22.3
Tanzania	**242**	35.3
Kenya	**360**	**41.3**

Source: World Bank 2006a.

Box 6.1

Negative Attitudes toward Women in the High Court

We should not be forgetful of historical truths that the action of women on our destiny has been and is unceasing, and that since the Great Fall in the Garden, woman has continued to baffle. We recall that through women's incitement, mankind was banished and doomed to die . . . .[a]

a. High Court judge, in a division of matrimonial property case, HCCC no. 1610/95, *Beatrice Kimani v. Evanson Njoroge.*

Box 6.2

Examples of Customary Justice

- Shortly after Emily Owino's husband died, her in-laws took all her possessions—including farm equipment, livestock, householder goods, and clothing. The in-laws insisted that she be "cleansed" by having sex with a social outcast, a custom in her region, as a condition of staying in her home. They paid a herdsman to have sex with Emily, against her will and without a condom. They later took over her farmland. She sought help from the local elder, who did nothing. Her in-laws forced her out of her home, and she and her children were homeless until someone offered her a small leaky shack. No longer able to afford school fees, her children dropped out of school.
- Lydiah Wanza, a 37-year-old Kamba widow, told an elder that her brothers-in-law took her land in Meru when her husband died. The elder "kept quiet and said he would answer later, but nothing happened."

Source: Human Rights Watch 2003.

Government of Kenya–Led Reform Efforts Are Underway

The government of Kenya's Governance, Justice, Law and Order Sector (GJLOS) Reform Programme was launched in November 2003 and will be implemented over five years. It is a multidonor- and government-funded initiative aimed at fundamentally reforming justice delivery in Kenya (box 6.3).

Gender is described as a crosscutting theme in the GJLOS Reform Programme (box 6.4).

Although the program is in its early stages, a number of encouraging initiatives have already taken place to address the issue of gender equality in justice delivery (box 6.5).

A particular problem faced by women seeking to enforce their legal rights, particularly in the lower courts, is the limited knowledge and misinterpretation of formal family, property, and succession laws. The GJLOS Reform Programme is funding the National Council for Law Reporting, which has the potential to bring increased transparency into the system in this respect through the publication of formal law reports (box 6.6).

The 12 female judges in the High Court are important drivers of change. They are all members of the Kenya Women Judges Association,

Box 6.3

GJLOS Vision for Improved Justice Service Delivery

The key aims of the GJLOS Reform Programme are

- responsive and enforceable policy, law, and regulation;
- more effective GJLOS institutions;
- reduced corruption-related impunity;
- improved access to justice, especially for the poor, marginalized, and vulnerable; and
- more informed and participative citizenry and nonstate actors.

Source: Government of Kenya 2005c.

Box 6.4

What the GJLOS Reform Programme Says about Gender

... In order to respond effectively to the needs of a society in transition, the programme will support the development and operationalization of laws, policies, regulations and initiatives that seek to enhance democracy, gender equity, human rights and governance e.g. ... a GJLOS gender policy ....

A key GJLOS reform priority is to further engender the legal and policy framework in Kenya by removing gender-biased discriminatory legislation, policies and regulations and the promotion of gender-sensitive, pro-poor laws, policies and regulations that afford other vulnerable groups, and women in particular, their rightful place as equal participants in society through effective policy implementation. In particular, the programme will support human rights and gender-sensitive initiatives in non-state institutions.

Source: Government of Kenya 2005c.

which has undertaken training for both judges and magistrates on gender issues, including on the application of international conventions on Kenya's domestic laws. So far about half the judiciary has received such training.

Box 6.5

Initiatives Are Taking Place across the Sector to Improve Justice Service Delivery to Women

- The Kenya Police have held culture and attitude seminars. Child Protection and Gender Desks have been introduced. About 60 officers have been trained specifically in gender issues.
- About 6,000 government-appointed local officials—chiefs and assistant chiefs—have received training that has included children's rights, succession, and land issues. A performance appraisal system has been put in place.
- Members of District Land Tribunals, responsible for dealing with certain types of land disputes in accordance with customary law, have received structured training, including on gender issues.
- A proposed National Legal Aid scheme, involving both civil society organizations and lawyers supplying pro bono services, has the potential, if implemented, to enhance women's access to justice.

Source: GJLOS 2005; also interviews with GJLOS staff.

Box 6.6

Law Reporting Makes the Law More Transparent

The National Council for Law Reporting is a corporate body established under the National Council for Law Reporting Act of 1994. Its mandate is to publish the *Kenya Law Reports*, containing judgments, rulings, and opinions of the superior courts of record, and to undertake such other publications as in the opinion of the Council are reasonably related to, or connected with, the preparation and publication of the reports. The Council hopes to be able to publish the laws of Kenya in electronic form. It has already established a Web site (www.kenyalaw.com) on which can be found judicial opinions from the Court of Appeal and the High Court and which is a forum for the publication of articles and commentaries on contemporary legal issues.

Source: GJLOS 2005.

Civil Society Organizations Are Having an Impact

There are a number of initiatives taking place outside government that seek to improve the quality of decision making at the community level, including in relation to issues of gender (box 6.7). Not only do civil society organizations campaign for improved legal rights for women, but they also undertake effective work on the ground—for example, through field officers working directly with communities to assist them in resolving disputes. Women's groups can be important channels for reaching communities to enhance knowledge about legal rights (for example, FIDA's "ABC of

---

Box 6.7

Initiatives to Improve Justice for Women

FIDA (Kenya) was founded in 1985 and now receives funding from a variety of donors. It provides vital legal support to women and is a powerful lobby group. FIDA employs full-time lawyers in its Nairobi and Kisumu offices. Its programs focus on legal aid, legal reform, advocacy, monitoring of human rights and violations, reporting on the status and rights of women, police training, and domestic violence issues. Specific activities include training of community and opinion leaders, spreading legal awareness, and taking up public interest cases. FIDA's paralegal training takes place mainly in rural areas. Potential paralegals are selected with O-level grades, plus Swahili and English. They have regular training and are given certificates. FIDA has also produced an "ABC of Property Law," which enables women to know their rights and contains simplified procedures on how to enforce them.

International Commission of Jurists: Kenya Section has the mandate to promote and protect the rule of law and democracy to ultimately secure all human rights for all Kenyans. ICJ has run projects to strengthen the legal protection and enforcement of women's property and inheritance rights.

Education Centre for Women in Democracy undertakes civic education on women's rights. It has trained paralegals who concentrate on women's property and inheritance rights and widows' rights.

Centre for Rights Education and Awareness began operations in 1999 and provides legal services, counseling, shelter to victims, community awareness, and advocates for legislative change. It runs a legal aid clinic in Nairobi, but also undertakes outreach work in other areas.

Property Law," which sets out in straightforward terms what women's rights are and how to enforce them).[1]

Recommendations

Immediately

- Strengthen gender mainstreaming within the GJLOS Reform Programme (implementation led by the Ministry of Justice and Constitutional Affairs), including the following:
  - Strengthen training for judges, magistrates, chiefs, and police on laws relating to women's property rights, women's rights in general, and their responsibility to enforce those laws.
  - Publicize High Court decisions confirming women's inheritance and property rights and ensure that they are applied in the Magistrates Courts through monitoring decisions on a "spot-check" basis.
  - Ensure that the GJLOS monitoring and evaluation system includes sex-disaggregated data to enable impact of justice reforms on women to be assessed.

In the Longer Term

- Ensure that the proposed national legal aid system (developing within GJLOS) adequately addresses gender issues, strengthens community-based justice by equipping NGO community-based field workers with tools and techniques to mediate disputes in a gender-sensitive manner, and trains community leaders to do the same.

Note

1. In a study of civil education by USAID in 1997, women's groups were found to be one of the most important avenues to reach communities (Thalman 1997).

CHAPTER 7

The Impact and Opportunities of International Trade and Labor

The women make these baskets, but they don't have the market. We want to find them a market.

—Zohra Baraka, Mohazo Ex-Impo Ltd.,
Voices of Women Entrepreneurs in Kenya

The Kenyan Ministry of Trade and Industry is already demonstrating leadership in its commitment to recognizing the links between trade policy, equitable growth, and gender issues. The Ministry of Trade and Industry commissioned a gender review of the World Bank Group IDA/MSME value chain projects associated with key exports (coffee, pyrethrum, and cotton-to-garment), and it is maintaining contact with export-oriented women's business associations such as OWIT Kenya. Kenya is today one of only two African countries with an active local chapter of the Organization of Women in International Trade (OWIT), and encouragement from OWIT promoted the creation of the Gender Unit in the Ministry of Trade and Industry. The Gender Unit has a staff of four and is tasked to engage with civil society women's groups and women business owners wishing to export. Ddamilura and Abdi (2003) note the work done in Kenya and Uganda by Trade Ministry officials to foster trust and collaboration with civil society groups.

Box 7.1

Kenya and International Trade

Since 1999, there has been a significant increase in the total value of Kenya's exports because of improved international commodity prices, with exports now accounting for 25 percent of Kenya's GDP. Kenya's principal merchandise exports are horticultural products (especially cut flowers), tea, coffee, and pyrethrum. For services exports, tourism receipts are critical to the Kenyan economy, generating US$494 million in 2004 (almost as much as horticultural exports). African countries account for almost half of Kenya's exports. The main markets for Kenya are the European Union (EU), Uganda, and Tanzania. The largest sources of Kenya's imports are the European Union, the United Arab Emirates, and South Africa.

Kenya receives preferential access to developed-country markets under a variety of schemes, including the Generalized System of Preferences (GSP) and extensions to it such as the U.S. African Growth and Opportunity Act (AGOA). As a signatory of the Lomé Convention and the later Cotonou Agreement, Kenya is eligible for tariff preferences in the EU market. Kenya is also party to two regional trade agreements: the Common Market for Eastern and Southern Africa (COMESA) and the East African Community (EAC). Kenya is one of very few countries now recognizing the importance of gender analysis as a variable in trade policy and is now attempting to include women's groups in the decision-making processes.

Gender Influences the Impact of International Trade

International trade has had not only a positive impact on Kenya's economy (box 7.1) but also a significant impact on gender equality, particularly for export industries (where the majority of employees are women). As discussed later in this chapter, women make up between 65 and 75 percent of workers in the cut flower sector, more than three-quarters of workers in the textiles sector, and about a third of the estimated workforce in tourism.

Trade Liberalization Can Attract Foreign Investment and Has Resulted in Increased Employment Opportunities for Women

International trade has opened up new opportunities in Kenya's formal labor force for women, who predominate in the workforce of important export sectors such as coffee, cut flowers, and textiles. Trade liberalization typically results in an increase in labor-intensive exports from developing countries. Many of these industries tend to be dominated by female workers often employed for their manual dexterity. As a result, higher exports are frequently accompanied by significant increases in female employment in the formal sector. Women employed in the production of manufactures for export typically earn more than they would have in traditional and informal sectors, leading to their improved status and bargaining power within their households.

New Employment Opportunities Bring Both New Challenges and Opportunities

Despite the advantages, trade liberalization is often coupled with persistent occupational segregation by sex, both vertical and horizontal (Randriamaro 2005). Increased trade can both widen and decrease gender wage gaps. On one hand, trade often rewards most those workers with greater skills. If women lack skills relative to men, this may increase the likelihood that women will be employed as temporary workers, with increased job insecurity and less ability to negotiate wages or other working conditions. On the other hand, increased international competition can put pressure on firms to cut costs, resulting in less discrimination against women with similar skills to men. In countries like Kenya where wages in the Export Processing Zones (EPZs) are above the minimum wage, research indicates a narrowing impact of increased trade and foreign direct investment on the occupational gender wage gap for low-skilled occupations (figure 7.1).

In rural areas, with a shift to cash crops for export, women are often worse off because of their double work burden. Women not only have ongoing responsibility for household food security, but their additional paid labor is often mediated through their husbands or other male family members—who also receive the remuneration (Baden 1998). The implications of this are not always addressed in either macro or sectoral interventions. For example, the World Bank Group IDA/MSME coffee value chain project was measuring positive development impact through increase in household incomes and additional jobs created for female workers (usually as pickers). But a gender analysis revealed that the women themselves could see little benefit because the money for their extra labor was paid directly to their husbands—most often the cooperative member—and the extra income did not always find its way back to the family. Cigarettes, alcohol, and the ability to purchase additional wives were cited.[1] For female-headed households, the lack of direct access

Figure 7.1. Occupational Gender Wage Gap versus FDI Net Inflows, by Country[a]

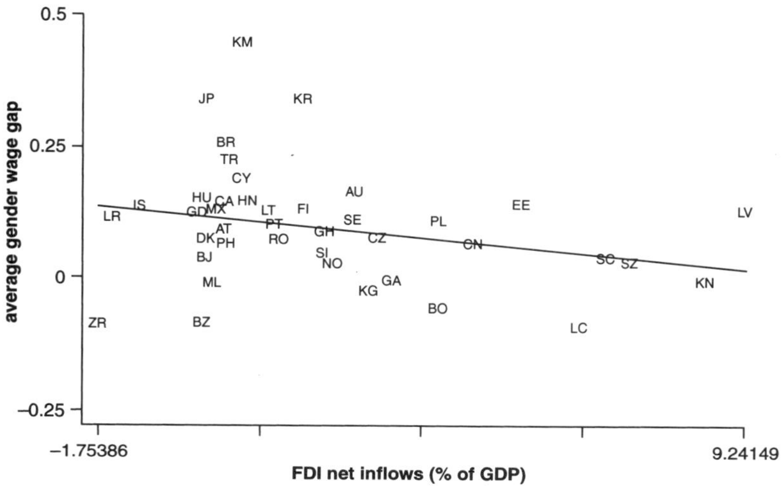

Source: Oostendrop 2004
a. Country key: AG-Antigua and Barbuda; AN-Netherlands Antilles; AS-American Samoa; AU-Australia; BJ-Benin; BO-Bolivia; BR-Brazil; BY-Belarus; CA-Canada; CN-China; CS-Czechoslovakia; CY-Cyprus; CZ-Czech Republic; DK-Denmark; EE-Estonia; FI-Finland; GA-Gabon; GB-United Kingdom; GH-Ghana; GI-Gibraltar; GP-Guadeloupe; HK-Hong Kong (China); HN-Honduras; HU-Hungary; IM-Isle of Man; IS-Iceland; JP-Japan; KG-Kyrgyz Republic; KM-Comoros; KN-St. Kitts and Nevis; KR- Republic of Korea; LC-St. Lucia; LT-Lithuania; LU-Luxembourg; LV-Latvia; MO-Macau (China); MU-Mauritius; NO-Norway; PE-Peru; PL-Poland; PR-Puerto Rico; PT-Portugal; RO-Romania; RU-Russian Federation; SC-Seychelles; SE-Sweden; SG-Singapore; SI-Slovenia; SK-Slovak Republic; SZ-Swaziland; TR-Turkey; US-United States; VI-Virgin Islands (U.S.); ZR-Democratic Republic of Congo (formerly Zaire).

to resources such as land, credit, or cooperative membership creates additional hurdles to deriving benefits from trade liberalization.

Significant Gender Discrimination Exists in Kenya's Formal Labor Market

Women in Kenya are well represented in the labor market. More than 88 percent of men and 78 percent of women are in the labor force (Government of Kenya 2005b). But gender discrimination persists in the formal sector because (a) women make up only 29 percent of the formal labor force (UNDP 2002), (b) women's earnings are on average 58 percent lower than men's (World Bank 2003e), and (c) women and men are occupationally segmented. These differences result from a number of factors, including more investment in the human capital of sons than of daughters, employers with discriminatory preferences about whom to hire and pay more, women's dominant role in raising children and maintaining the household, and sociocultural norms that restrict women's ability to work outside the home and in certain sectors (for example, fishing and night work).

Discriminatory and Outdated Labor Laws Fail to Address Gender Issues and Decrease Women's Ability to Fully Benefit from International Trade

Employment laws in Kenya date from before independence and are generally inadequate to regulate its modern labor market. New labor laws are being developed. The International Labour Organization has worked with the Ministry of Labour and Human Resource Development to produce six new employment laws to replace the existing framework and provide Kenya with modern employment standards. The drafting was completed in April 2004, and the draft bills are currently with the government's Legislative Drafting Department and are awaiting the approval of the Labour Advisory Board. Key gender-related issues not adequately addressed in the current laws, but provided for in the proposed new laws, include prohibitions on women undertaking inappropriate work (for example, Employment Act restrictions on night work), discrimination (for example, in relation to wages and maternity leave), and sexual harassment in the workplace.

The proposed Employment Rights Act includes far-reaching provisions against discrimination in the workplace and in relation to employment policies and practices. Discrimination is widely defined to include any distinction, policy, or preference made on the basis of gender. Maternity leave provisions are also addressed, providing for statutory maternity leave and pay. The proposed new laws provide a comprehensive code defining and dealing with sexual harassment, including the requirement for every employer employing not less than 20 employees to issue a policy statement.

Female Entrepreneurs Have Yet to Fully Benefit from International Trade

For female entrepreneurs, inequalities in access to resources (such as land and credit) and the ability to control the additional income generated by trade can determine whether benefits will accrue to them. If women have inferior access, they are less likely to benefit from the opportunities that trade brings. A study of tea growers in Kenya between 1975 and 1982 found that even though nearly one-third of rural households were headed by women and most of the labor involved in tea picking was done by women and girls, female-headed households had only half the propensity of male-headed households to adopt tea growing (Bevan, Collier, and Gunning 1989). Women's inferior access to land, extension, and credit, as well as the size of female-headed households (which tend to be smaller than average), may have constrained them from adopting tea cultivation (World Bank 2004b).

Most female exporters in Kenya specialize in sectors such as handicrafts, curios, and horticultural products. Since 2002, Kenyan knitwear, handwoven baskets, wood carvings, and stone curios have yielded significant export earnings. For example, Kenana Knitters, which produces woven rugs and carpets and employs 200 women, directly increased its exports from US$1,116 in 2002 to US$110,970 in 2004 (Chemengich and Gale 2005). But competition in production has increased because of the development of synthetic substitutes and machine-made crafts that are being manufactured more cheaply by other countries, particularly in South Asia. A particular challenge is the protection of intellectual property. Products based on traditional knowledge that belong to communities are not easily protected under the WTO's Agreement on Trade-Related Aspects of Intellectual Property Rights. Consequently, some Kenyan products have been copied and granted intellectual property protection elsewhere. One example is traditional handwoven Kenyan baskets: the machine used to produce them has been patented in Korea.

With limited domestic demand, both female and male entrepreneurs will have to diversify their products and increase value added to break into new markets. To identify new markets, female entrepreneurs need access to trade-related information and to participate in (expensive and often male-dominated) trade promotion missions. Many women exporters also face capacity constraints. To secure orders in new markets and develop credibility, women must be able to supply, on time, consistent quantities of quality products. This requires access to credit and know-how. Some female-owned businesses in Kenya have coordinated efforts (for example, the National Handloom Weavers Association) to supply large orders in foreign markets. This could be replicated by other sectors and other women's groups.

Carr's case studies suggest that regional trading arrangements are likely to offer opportunities that are best suited to women as predominantly small-scale producers and traders, given proximity of neighboring markets, more readily available information, and contacts (Carr 2004). In the longer term, the growing commitment from U.S.-based multinational corporations to supplier diversity, including sourcing from women- and minority-owned businesses, may well benefit women in the supply chain in developing countries such as Kenya. The Women's Business Enterprise National Council (WBENC) has been asked by its corporate customers to explore ways of certifying women business owners offshore. This could have obvious positive implications for women entrepreneurs as part of global supply chains. The Ministry of Trade and Industry's Gender Unit and groups like OWIT Kenya could play a useful convening role to help facilitate this process.

Trade in Textiles, Cut Flowers, and Tourism: Impacts on Employment, Wages, and Working Conditions for Women in Kenya

The textiles, cut flowers, and tourism sectors in Kenya have experienced high growth in exports and use female labor intensively. The case studies below illustrate that in these sectors there have been significant impacts for women in employment, remuneration, and working conditions. Addressing gender inequalities in these sectors is essential because not only do women make up a significant share of employees but also international buyers and investors are increasingly demanding that companies do so. For example, socially responsible investors such as the Calvert Group are arguing that there is a clear relationship between gender equality and economic development and that corporations have a role to play in redressing gender imbalances.

The Textiles and Clothing Sector

Following its dramatic decline in the 1990s, brought about by trade liberalization and the resulting competition from imports of new and secondhand clothing,[2] Kenya's textile and clothing sector has made a strong recovery in recent years on the back of increased exports to the United States under AGOA preferences. Kenya's textile and clothing sales to the United States increased from US$39.5 million in 1999 to US$277 million in 2004, with employment in the sector growing from 26,000 in 2002 to 37,000 in 2003 (dropping to 35,000 by the end of 2004).

The largest new investments in Kenya's textile and clothing sector are taking place within its Export Processing Zones (EPZs), introduced in

Table 7.1. Performance of Textiles and Clothing Firms in Kenya's EPZs

	2000	2001	2002	2003	2004	2005
Number of firms	6	17	30	35	30	25
Employment	6,487	12,002	25,288	36,348	34,614	34,234
Investment						
(US$ millions)	15.7	47.9	87.8	127.9	108.4	120.0
Exports (US$ millions)	30.2	54.6	103.5	146.0	221.6	208.0

Source: EPZA 2005b.

1990 to initiate industrialization based on shifting the economy away from import substitution toward export promotion (table 7.1).[3] Exports from the EPZs now account for almost 10.75 percent of Kenya's total exports and 2.19 percent of GDP. Textiles is the dominant sector in the EPZs, accounting for more than 40 percent of firms, 91.5 percent of employment, and 73 percent of sales.

Women account for more than three-quarters of workers in the sector and are often employed in low-skilled jobs such as sewing and finishing. Most are young women, either recent school leavers, using the work to provide income before continuing with their education, or single mothers. In contrast, men employed in the sector are generally older (30–40 years old) and often act as supervisors. Female employees in the textiles sector are often the most important income earners in their families, most notably in the Athi River area. Increased trade in textiles has, therefore, helped women improve their welfare and decision-making power within the household. Most EPZs recruit from the local communities and retrain the workers. The catchment areas for the majority of the EPZs are the informal areas (often slums) that border them and are home to more than 80 percent of urban residents (Chemengich and Gale 2005).

Yet there has been a perception that workers in Kenya's EPZs, particularly female textile workers, face poor working conditions and low pay. However, both working conditions and wages appear to have improved following, in particular, the industrial unrest witnessed in 2003, which led to the development of collective bargaining agreements. Other factors have also had an impact:

- **Market-driven checks.** Increased concerns of final consumers in northern markets regarding labor standards in producing countries have forced firms in the EPZs to improve working conditions. Factory inspections examine the working environments of firms in the EPZs on a regular basis, and all foreign buyers audit firms to certify them before placing orders.

- **Minimum wage laws.** Although the textiles and spinning sector pays the lowest wages in Kenya's EPZs (figure 7.2), their wages are similar to those in the informal sector and must comply with minimum wage laws. The current wage structure is 12.5–25 percent above the minimum wage, and textile workers receive more than the lowest salary paid in the Kenyan civil service. Wages in Kenya's EPZs are also increasing, rising on average by 40 percent between 2001 and 2004.
- **Training opportunities.** Women also benefit from on-the-job and other training opportunities, which help improve their productivity, as well as the competitiveness of the sector. In Kenya's EPZs, there is in-house training for female workers in stitching, sewing, cutting, screen printing, and garment washing. A number of initiatives are promoting awareness about HIV/AIDS (box 7.2).

Challenges ahead. The textiles sector in Kenya faces challenges. Employment by firms located in the EPZs actually fell (by 6 percent) between 2003 and 2005 because of the closure of 10 textile firms.[4] The closures came as a response to the end of the WTO Agreement on Textiles and Clothing,[5] forcing Kenya to compete with lower-cost production from China and India, and as a result of the relatively high costs of doing business in Kenya, principally for power and infrastructure.[6]

Figure 7.2. Wages in Kenya's EPZs Are Lowest for Textiles and Spinning, but Similar to Those in the Informal Sector

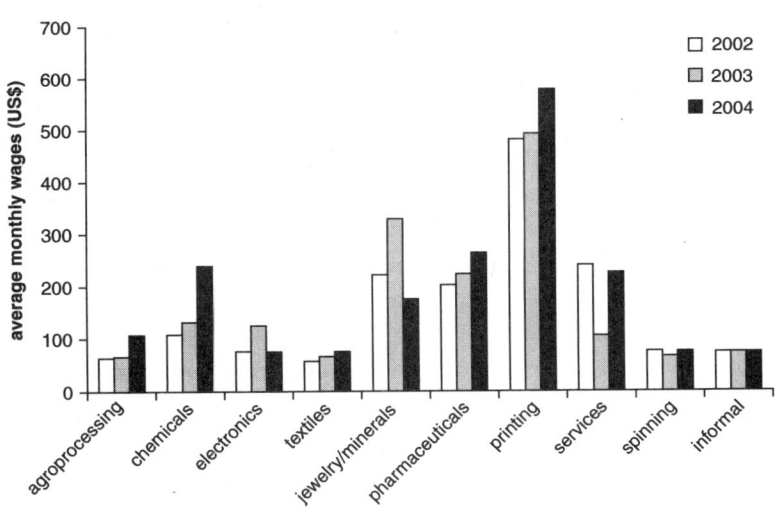

Source: EPZA 2005a.

Box 7.2

Alltex EPZ: An Example of Best Practices in Female Worker Policies

The Alltex EPZ Limited plant in the Export Processing Zone at Athi River has created employment for more than 2,000 Kenyans, more than 80 percent of whom are women. The plant, one of the largest textile factories in the zone, is a joint venture between the Industrial Promotion Services (an affiliate of the Aga Khan Fund for Economic Development) and the Global Readymade Garments Industry LLC (Qatar), with an annual turnover of US$35 million. The facility is the only establishment in the EPZ and the region so far that has provided a day nursery for working mothers with infants to be cared for while they are at work. Alltex has also pioneered social service programs for HIV/AIDS sufferers, which have now been expanded to cover 20 companies in the EPZ.

Moreover, AGOA benefits are likely to disappear as the market liberalizes, including the U.S. market. In particular, more flexible rules of origin for Kenya's[7] exports of textiles and clothing to the United States under AGOA (in particular, clothing made from imported yarn or manufactured from imported textiles is eligible) are scheduled to become more rigorous after September 2007. Producers will then be required to utilize locally or regionally produced textiles in the production of garments to avoid compromising the AGOA-eligibility status of the finished garment. There are doubts as to whether these options are currently feasible for Kenya's apparel producers. High-quality fabric and yarn are available from the United States, but sourcing them to make clothing will at least double the unit cost and make them uncompetitive. And although Kenya has a cotton-textiles-clothing supply chain, only the garments part of it is thriving and competitive. All other parts of the chain (for example, cotton production) currently lack adequate capacity. The option for sourcing fabric and yarn from other AGOA-eligible countries is also limited by regional supply constraints. Moreover, the fabric produced locally and regionally fails to meet the variety and quality demanded by the U.S. market (Ikiara and Ndirangu 2003), although a few Kenyan firms are showing early successes in exporting high-fashion embroidered products that attract higher value. It will therefore be crucial for Kenya to develop local and regional cotton-textiles supply chains and for women workers in the textiles sector to upgrade their skills.

The Cut Flowers Sector

Cut flowers have become Kenya's second-largest agricultural export (after tea), generating more than US$200 million yearly in foreign exchange earnings (half of Kenya's horticultural exports and 14 percent of the country's total exports), and employing 70,000 people directly[8] and more than 500,000 indirectly. In recent years, production has grown by 20 percent annually (box 7.3). Women have benefited from the

---

Box 7.3

Reaching the Export Market for Flowers

Elizabeth Thande, the managing director of Wet Farm Ltd., owns a flower farm situated on 28 acres of family land that specializes in the production of cut flowers, including Arabicum and Gladiolus varieties. Ms. Thande sells her varieties mainly at flower auctions in Holland and at a few direct markets in France, the Middle East, and the United Kingdom. The Dutch flower auctions have historically been the most important channel through which Kenyan flower exports are distributed, although in several EU markets supermarkets are beginning to dominate as importers (EPZA 2005a). She notes that access to the international markets is the key issue for sustaining her business. She has attended international fairs and exhibitions in Europe, Latin America, and the United States. For Ms. Thande, these are the "most effective tools for information exchange and marketing."

Keeping up to date with the market needs is also a challenge. "In this trade, you have to do a lot of market studies. The flower industry is like a fashion industry; it keeps on changing. You have to be always aware of the market," she says. To find out about market trends, she is part of several associations, including the Fresh Produce Exporters Association of Kenya and the African Women in Agribusiness, which provide her with technical information on production, grading, and packaging. "The horticulture industry is a very technical field. These are areas where we need a lot of technical assistance and training," she says.

Her biggest competitors are the multinational companies, which are "able to use the best technology and have bigger volume." Elizabeth plans to move away from the auction market and sell her flowers directly to the buyers. "Most of our flowers end up on the American market through the Dutch auctions. This is why we think it is time for us to go directly to the American market." She attended an exhibition in March 2006 in Miami and is considering financing options for expanding her business.

strong growth of the sector in Kenya, making up between 65 and 75 percent of its workers. More than half of the workers have migrated from areas of the country where there are higher levels of unemployment.

A rigid division of labor has resulted in women being concentrated in the most labor-intensive production processes that are important for the cosmetic quality of the final product. These include picking, packing, and value added processing activities, which require intense concentration and long periods of standing. Men, on the other hand, are primarily employed in management (including supervision) and in physical tasks (such as spraying, irrigation, construction, and cold storage). The industry employs mainly young workers, who are better suited to the labor-intensive nature of the work. More than half of female employees are 20–24 years old (Dolan, Opondo, and Smith 2002). Although wages are low,[9] they are higher than the minimum wage. Companies also provide employees with housing or a housing allowance (equivalent to 15–30 percent of the basic wage).

However, the industry has been plagued by allegations of poor labor practices and reports of sexual harassment against female workers by male supervisors in packhouses and greenhouses, although this is often viewed as a cultural rather than a sector issue. Women frequently face difficult working conditions, with long working hours and job insecurity. On many farms, overtime is compulsory and is particularly common for packers at certain times of the year (for example, Valentine's Day), when there is pressure to meet large orders. At such times, it is common for pickers and packers to work 16–18 hours per day. Female workers are often involved in overtime work (because they form the majority of packers), which can have serious implications (particularly in the absence of suitable childcare arrangements), because they typically also bear the responsibility for household and domestic tasks.

Consumers have responded by placing increasing pressure on floriculture companies to account for the social and environmental impacts of their operations. Changes in market regulations in the European Union and United States have called for stricter standards in traceability, quarantine, packaging, recycling, and labor practices. Concerns about commercial losses have prompted flower traders and producers to develop their own codes of conduct. Consequently, floriculture in Kenya has become one of the most codified agricultural sectors in the world. By the mid-1990s, most of the largest producers had applied codes of conduct to gain or maintain market access by satisfying the requirements of consumers, although many of the smaller growers were forced to close because of the costs of compliance. Because the European Union is the main market for the Kenyan flower industry, it governs the quality standards for the sector. These are extremely strict and costly to the sector, but they have led flower companies in Kenya to institute a number of positive changes of particular benefit to women workers, including health and safety measures, maternity-leave benefits, and improved industrial relations.

Tourism

Tourism is an important sector of the Kenyan economy and a large source of formal and informal employment for women. Tourism earnings increased significantly between 2003 and 2004, from US$340 million (2.3 percent of GDP) to US$494 million (3.1 percent of GDP). International arrivals grew by 18.7 percent—from 1,146,100 to 1,360,700—over the same period (Government of Kenya 2005a). About 78 percent of the major hotels on the coast and about 66 percent of those in Nairobi have some foreign investment, although less than 20 percent are owned entirely by foreigners (Christie and Crompton 2001). Yet growth over the longer term has been erratic. Fierce competition for tourists and overdevelopment of tourist facilities have created downward pressure on prices, progressively edging out luxury tourism through deterioration in quality. Crime has also had a considerable impact on the sector, and estimates indicate that travel advisories have cost the country nearly US$200 million in recent years (World Bank 2006c).

Tourism accounts for 138,000 jobs in the formal sector (45,000 of which are held by women) and, through its links to domestic industries, 360,000 jobs in the informal sector (the majority of which are held by females involved in the sale of handicrafts such as weaving and wooden carvings) (Ikiara 2001). The seasonal nature of tourism, which is influenced by demand and weather changes, is an important factor in tourism performance and results in employment instability that reduces the sector's employment benefits for women. On average, 25 percent of hotel employees are usually laid off during the low season (English 1986).

Women entrepreneurs have yet to fully benefit from Kenya's booming tourism sector. Although women are engaged in curios, as clothes sellers, or as beauty salon owners, they are less often found in the hotel industry or as tour operators. Interviews with women entrepreneurs reveal that the high start-up capital needed for such ventures is too prohibitive for them, and as a result women entrepreneurs remain largely confined to small-scale activities.

The Kenyan government is now working to attract upmarket tourists. Programs include consultations with airlines that had abandoned Kenya as a destination, marketing of new tourist sites and products (for example, sports tourism), exploration of new tourist markets (for example, East Asia), promotion of domestic tourism, and public-private partnerships in marketing the country abroad as a tourist destination.

Recommendations

Immediately

- The Central Bureau of Statistics, the Ministry of Trade and Industry, and the Ministry of Planning should enhance its collection and reporting of sex-disaggregated data to facilitate more detailed research into the impact of trade on gender relations and the livelihoods of women in Kenya.
- The Ministry of Trade and Industry should continue to strengthen its capacity to recognize the gender-differentiated impacts of trade liberalization and ensure integration of systematic gender analysis in trade policy making and negotiations; continue to engage with women's business associations (WBAs) and civil society stakeholders to ensure their involvement in, and input to, Kenya's trade policy making and promotional efforts; and promote gender awareness and social responsibility through appropriate engagement with the private sector.
- WBAs should ensure that they take the opportunity offered to be engaged and regularly interact with the Ministry of Trade and Industry to increase their understanding of relevant issues.
- IFC, OWIT, and the Commonwealth Secretariat should facilitate capacity building to Ministry of Trade and Industry officials and WBAs on the linkages between international trade and gender and on the practical tools available to assist women entrepreneurs in accessing trade-related information and training.

In the Longer Term

- The Ministry of Labour and Human Resource Development should undertake regulatory impact assessments on proposed new labor laws, including a gender assessment. In particular, there is a need to ensure that the proposed new maternity provisions will not have the unintended consequence of excluding women from the workplace.
- The Ministry of Labour and Human Resource Development, the Ministry of Trade and Industry, and the Ministry of Education should make

efforts to upgrade skills, training, capacity building, and economic literacy for export-oriented women entrepreneurs and review the industrial training levy scheme. Trade development offices in all districts (under the Ministry of Trade and Industry) should be used more effectively for women entrepreneurs to access information and training.

• Kenyan entrepreneurs need to be trained in how to patent their designs.

Notes

1. November 2005 discussions with project management.

2. Kenya's textile manufacturers supply 45 percent of the domestic textile market.

3. Firms located in Kenya's EPZs benefit from a number of incentives, including 10-year tax holidays (and thereafter lower corporate tax rates), exemptions from duty and value added tax (VAT) on imports of capital equipment and raw materials, and exemptions from various other taxes.

4. The textile firms that closed during the period were Tristar, Kenap, Indigo Garments, Kentex, Asia Resources, Ancheneyer, Birch, Match Point, Chandhu, and Sahara Stitch.

5. Which became effective on January 1, 2005.

6. The high cost of energy is a key constraint for the textiles sector in Kenya, averaging US$0.07 per kilowatt hour, compared with US$0.03–0.04 per kilowatt hour in competing countries such as South Africa and the Arab Republic of Egypt.

7. Together with those African countries defined as "lesser-developed"—not only least-developed countries, but all African countries except Mauritius and South Africa.

8. Employment is similar to that in the coffee (60,000) and tea (77,000) sectors.

9. In 2002, average wages were in the range of US$31–46 per month, with little variation between permanent and temporary (seasonal) employees.

CHAPTER 8

The Way Forward: Ensuring That Women's Voices Are Heard

We need to start an association that will be connected to our government that will enhance the processes, make them simpler, shorter, and smooth.

—Patience Nyaoga, Tintoria Laundry,
Voices of Women Entrepreneurs in Kenya

The recommendations in this GGA are policy-based and designed to bring about lasting, strategic change that will increase the economic power of women for Kenya's long-term growth. To accomplish this, there must be capacity at the national level to make the recommendations a reality, and the recommendations must be integrated into the government of Kenya's ongoing reform processes. Potentially the most important of these, as far as private sector development is concerned, is the Private Sector Development Strategy (PSDS), which sets out government's policy and medium-term priorities for achieving the objective of private sector–led growth in Kenya. Other entry points for reform include the GJLOS Reform Programme, the Financial and Legal Sector Technical Assistance Project, the National Commission on Gender and Development, the World Bank Group's IDA MSME project, and the African Development Bank's GOWE program.

Institutional Framework: The National Machinery for Implementing Gender and Development Goals

The national machinery for implementing gender and development goals in Kenya comprises two main institutions: the Department of Gender in the Ministry of Gender, Sports, Culture and Social Services and the National Commission on Gender and Development.

The Ministry of Gender, Sports, Culture and Social Services

The Ministry of Gender, Sports, Culture and Social Services has the mandate of coordinating policy formulation and gender mainstreaming at the national level. The Ministry comprises four departments—the Departments of Social Services, Culture, Sports, and Gender—and the core functions of the Ministry include (a) promotion of welfare of the vulnerable groups, which include women, the aged, and the youth; (b) promotion of sports and other cultural activities; and (c) provision of reading materials and facilities through libraries (Government of Kenya 2006a).

Within the Ministry, the Gender Department is the government's arm to mainstream gender issues. The Gender Department was established in 2004, when it was elevated from a division within a department to a full department, in an attempt to improve its efficiency and effectiveness in integrating gender concerns into policy formulation, planning, and implementation. Its mandate includes formulation, implementation, and monitoring of policies on gender issues; coordination of gender-related activities and collection; and analysis and dissemination of sex-disaggregated data. Specifically, the Department is responsible for providing technical support to promote a range of mechanisms in gender mainstreaming, including Gender Desks in line ministries; task force and high-level advisory training for making gender analysis a requirement in action plans; and accountability mechanisms such as monitoring, evaluation, and reporting (Government of Kenya 2006a). Its vision is to "to be a leading organization in promoting equality among women, men, girls, and boys in all sectors at all levels of development" (Government of Kenya 2006a). However, the Department has only a small staff and lacks resources, which makes it Challenging to effectively carry out its ambitious vision.

In addition to the Gender Department, Gender Desks in other Kenyan line ministries are being created with the objective of assisting the national machinery in mainstreaming gender issues. However, although some of these desks have already been established (there is, for example, a Gender Desk within the Ministry of Trade and Industry and the Ministry of Labour, Small and Medium Enterprise Development), the Gender Desks have yet to be formally launched. Moreover, the Gender Desks are currently coordinated by the individual ministries and so often seem to be set up in an ad hoc manner, without clear guidelines on their exact roles or sufficient funding to carry out their activities. The National Commission on Gender and Development aims to streamline the process and is currently drafting terms of reference for setting up Gender Desks within the different ministries.

National Commission on Gender and Development

In keeping with the commitments made by the government when it presented its Third and Fourth Reports to the UN Committee on the Elimination of All Forms of Discrimination against Women in New York in January 2003, the National Commission on Gender and Development Act of 2003 was passed by Parliament in 2003. As a result, the National Commission on Gender and Development has been operational since 2004.

Housed in the Ministry of Gender, Sports, Culture and Social Services, the Commission's mandate includes legal reform, advocacy, providing advice on gender issues to government, and coordinating the various government agencies' efforts on gender issues (Government of Kenya 2000a, 2004a). In contrast to the Department of Gender and Development, with its focus on implementation, the Commission's role is focused on coordination. The Commission comprises 18 commissioners drawn from government and civil society; however, it does not have any full-time paid commissioners. In addition to the National Commission on Gender and Development, the Kenya National Commission of Human Rights has also been established through an Act of Parliament. One of its tasks is to observe the principle of impartiality and gender equity.

The Role of Civil Society

In addition to its national machinery, Kenya has a vibrant women's movement, which has an important role in advancing the gender agenda and assisting the national machinery in facilitating the implementation of gender policies. Within the women's movement, a variety of institutions focus on different sectors, such as NGOs focusing on gender and law (FIDA), women and microfinance (KWFT), women and employment (the National Association of Self-Employed Women of Kenya) (World Bank 2004a), as well as numerous organizations focusing on gender issues more broadly, such as the League of Kenya Women Voters and the National Council of Women of Kenya.

However, although these organizations are active in addressing gender issues, interactions between them and public policy makers have traditionally been weak (Government of Kenya 2004a). Moreover, interactions and coalitions have tended to arise within a sector in response to a certain phenomenon (for example, the need to get women represented in the constitution reform process resulted in the creation of the Kenya Women's Political Caucus), rather then across sectors (World Bank 2004a).

Building Capacity to Meet the Challenges Ahead

Although the Gender Department within the Ministry of Gender, Sports, Culture and Social Services seems well placed to advance the gender agenda, and the recent formation of the Commission on Gender in particular is a positive step, the challenge is now to equip these institutions with the needed resources and the capacity to fulfill their mandates effectively. Capacity building of civil society organizations could help strengthen interactions between the government and civil society organizations and ultimately contribute to a more effective implementation of the government's gender policies. Given that advocacy gains by the women's movement often are undermined by the fact that policy makers lack information and analysis on the economic benefits of gender equality, it would be useful if some of the capacity-building efforts focused on the links between gender equality and economic growth.

Incorporate GGA Recommendations in the Government of Kenya's Reform Processes

The Private Sector Development Strategy (PSDS) sets out government's policy and medium-term priorities for achieving the objective of private sector–led growth in Kenya. Ideally, the Strategy will be the tool for determining the government of Kenya's resource allocations to achieve this objective, through the medium-term expenditure framework.

The PSDS has been developed under the auspices of the Ministry of Trade and Industry. The PSDS is a wide-ranging document addressing issues that affect private sector development in Kenya, ranging from crime and insecurity to infrastructure (box 8.1 and figure 8.1)

Box 8.1

The Private Sector Development Strategy (PSDS) at a Glance

Mission: To achieve a fast-growing, competitive private sector, driving the creation of wealth and employment for Kenya.

Goal 1: Improve Kenya's business environment. Activities include improving infrastructure; addressing crime, insecurity, and corruption; enhancing public-private dialogue; and reducing legal, administrative, and regulatory barriers.

Goal 2: Increase economic growth through trade expansion. Activities include finalizing the trade strategy, revitalizing trade facilitation, and increasing access to trade finance.

Goal 3: Accelerate institutional transformation. Activities include promoting culture change in the public and private sectors and reforming public institutions for better service delivery to the private sector.

Goal 4: Improve productivity. Activities include enhancing labor productivity; improving productivity of capital; stimulating research and development activities; and promoting the adoption of modern, appropriate technology.

Goal 5: Develop entrepreneurship and indigenous enterprise. Activities include facilitating the development of new enterprises, improving access to capital, delivering best-practice models to spur evolution of Kenyan businesses, strengthening firm-to-firm and SME-to-market linkages, and making business associations more representative of MSMEs.

Encouragingly, the draft PSDS identifies gender as a crosscutting issue for private sector development in Kenya (box 8.2).

The draft PSDS states that it aims to "give women increased access to resources and opportunities to reduce gender disparities in participation in the private sector and achieve greater participation of women in the enterprise sector." The indicative actions identified to achieve this objective tend to be focused on interventions at the firm level; for example, "developing appropriate credit instruments for women entrepreneurs within Access to Finance subcomponent of the MSMEs Competitiveness Project" and "developing proposals for a creative and thriving cottage industry, assisting women entrepreneurs without interfering with their regular duties."

Figure 8.1. Positioning of the Private Sector Development Strategy, 2006–10

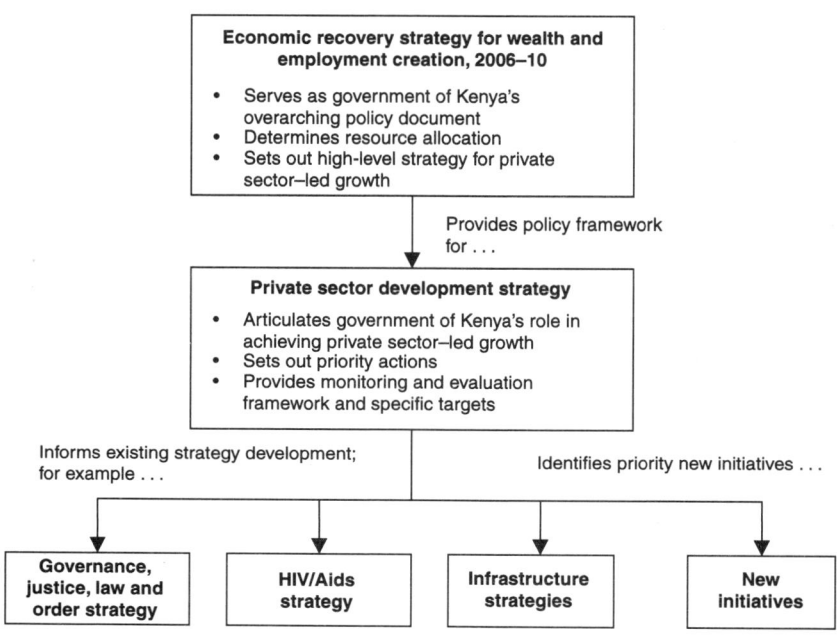

Source: Government of Kenya 2006b; Government of Kenya 2003b.

Box 8.2

What the PSDS Says about Gender

Economic experience over the past decades has clearly demonstrated that development is not only about economic growth, but it also embraces broader considerations, including promotion of equal opportunities among citizens, with equitable distributions of benefits.

The PSDS views gender mainstreaming as a crosscutting issue. The strategy takes account of gender equality concerns in all policy, program, administrative, and financial activities and in organization procedures, with a conscious attempt to eliminate gender bias. The PSDS will facilitate effective participation by women in the private sector.

Need for a "Joined-Up" Policy on PSD, with Gender Mainstreamed

There is a scope for strengthening the current PSDS in relation to gender issues. In particular, there is a need to move away from firm-level interventions to focus more on addressing the systemic, underlying issues that create barriers for female-owned businesses. Moreover, to operate effectively as the government of Kenya's agenda for private sector–led growth, the PSDS should encapsulate all current PSD policy initiatives and provide a coherent, prioritized, and sequenced framework for them. A number of initiatives to address PSD issues in Kenya exist, including the MSE Sessional Paper, the Ministry of Trade and Industry's Investment Climate Action Plan 2005–2007, the National Export Strategy Implementation Action Plan, and the Trade Policy Strategy. Some already include initiatives

---

Box 8.3

Gender Initiatives in the MSE Sessional Paper

The MSE Sessional Paper states that government of Kenya policy in relation to gender and MSEs is to do the following:

- Pursue gender-responsive policies that increase equal access to financial services by encouraging women to form SACCOs and by promoting their networking with MFIs and commercial banks.
- Promote women's access to education, technological development, and entrepreneurship, and also influence the orientation of women away from traditional activities to the production of nontraditional products that are more marketable and provide better remuneration.
- Build the institutional capacity of ministries and government departments for gender integration.
- Identify gender-related constraints and opportunities that affect equal participation of both genders at the local, institutional, and policy levels.
- In collaboration with the private sector, collect and provide sex-disaggregated data to facilitate gender-responsive planning and policy formulation.
- So that women's concerns are effectively mainstreamed into all MSE activities and women's participation enhanced, design all MSE programs and projects to ensure equal opportunities for women and men.
- Put into place a monitoring system that tracks the effects of government and donor activities on gender relations.

to address gender constraints on private sector development (box 8.3). There is already overlap, a plethora of priorities, and a limited coordination among them. The danger is that the PSDS could simply be added to the list of initiatives, rather than providing the overall framework for their coordination; where necessary, prioritizing between them; and providing a cohesive monitoring and evaluation framework.

Recommendations

The following are the specific recommendations to ensure that the PSDS appropriately addresses gender issues:

Immediately

- Include a clearly articulated policy statement in relation to government's role in achieving private sector–led growth and creating the environment to enhance women's contribution.
- Map the government of Kenya's ongoing PSD initiatives, including those relating to women, and develop a holistic framework for implementing them, including implementation structures and a monitoring and evaluation framework.
- Identify gaps not covered by current initiatives, such as the issues addressed by this GGA.
- In relation to each PSDS goal, consider gender-related barriers to achieving that goal and address them (for example, in the section on access to capital in the current document, the issue of women's limited access to capital is not discussed at all).
- The PSDS implementation arrangements, insofar as they involve the private sector, should ensure that there is representation from women entrepreneurs or groups representing them.
- The monitoring and evaluation arrangements for the PSDS should be designed to ensure that data are sex-disaggregated.
- The African Development Bank's GOWE program, managed by IFC PEP Africa, could work to strengthen women's businesses and associations to better advocate for needed change identified in this GGA.

In the Medium Term

Provide the National Commission on Gender and Development with the needed capacity and authority to ensure effective implementation of its mandate and to enable it to truly become an effective coordinating and advocacy body, including in relation to the gender dimensions of private sector issues.

List of Key Kenyan Organizations Focusing on Issues Covered in the GGA

Association of Media Women in Kenya (AMWIK)
This is a nonprofit national media association for women journalists from the print and electronic media and communications (www.amwik.org).

Association of Microfinance Institutions (AMFI)
Comprising 11 large MFIs serving more than 97,000 clients, AMFI's mission is to develop a microfinance industry and an institutional framework that serves poor and low-income people in Kenya (www.amfikenya.org).

International Federation of Women Lawyers (FIDA) Kenya
An organization that provides legal aid services, women's rights monitoring and advocacy, gender and legal rights awareness, and public relations and fundraising (http://www.fidakenya.org/).

Kenya Association of Manufacturers (KAM)
An organization that aims to promote competitive local manufacturing in liberalized markets, unite manufacturers, serve as a common voice for industry, and provide an essential link for cooperation, dialogue, and understanding with the government (http://www.kam.co.ke/default.asp).

Kenya Women Judges Association (KWJA)

An affiliate of the International Association of Women Judges, this organization promotes and encourages gender equality in all matters relating to the administration of justice (http://www.kwja.org/).

Kenya Bankers Association (KBA)

The association serves as a lobby for the banks' interests and addresses issues affecting member institutions (http://www.kenyabankersassociation.com/about.php).

Kenya Institute of Management (KIM)

This organization aims to enhance management knowledge and practice in both the public and private sectors. It has more than 4,000 individual members and about 500 corporate members (http://www.kim.ac.ke/about.html).

Kenya Land Alliance (KLA)

An umbrella network of civil society organizations and individuals committed to effective advocacy for the reform of policies and laws governing land in Kenya (http://www.kenyalandalliance.or.ke/aboutus.htm).

Kenya Law Reform Commission (KLRC)

Established on May 21, 1982, this is the primary agency to spearhead law reform and review processes in the country (no Web site, but some information appears at http://www.gjlos.go.ke/gjinner.asp?pcat2=agencies&pcat=minjust&cat=klrc).

Kenya National Commission for Human Rights (NCHR)

An independent national human rights institution (established by an Act of Parliament) whose core mandate is to further the protection and promotion of human rights in Kenya (http://www.knchr.org/section.asp?ID=1).

Kenya Private Sector Alliance (KEPSA)

KEPSA seeks to bring together the private sector representative organizations in Kenya, so that they can speak with a single voice to influence public policy formulation (http://www.kepsa.or.ke/index.html).

Kenya Women Entrepreneurs Board

A recently formed women's business association that aims to provide advice to women entrepreneurs and play an advocacy role on the issues that are inhibiting the development of their businesses.

Kenya Women Finance Trust (KWFT)

A microfinance institution that provides financial and nonfinancial services to low-income women entrepreneurs (http://www.kwft.org/about.asp).

Law Society of Kenya (LSK)

Kenya's premier bar association, with the mandate to advise and assist members of the legal profession, the government, and the larger public in all matters relating to the administration of justice in Kenya (http://www.lsk.or.ke/).

National Commission on Gender and Development

A recently formed commission with a mandate that includes legal reform, advocacy, providing advice on gender issues to government, and coordinating the various government agencies' efforts on gender issues.

National Council of Law Reporting (NCLR)

A corporate body that aims to provide the latest and most relevant case law and other legal information, with a view to promoting the teaching and practice of law, the delivery of justice, and the evolution of Kenya's jurisprudence.

National Land Policy Secretariat

Seeks to conduct a consultative process and produce a National Land Policy that will guide the country toward a sustainable and equitable use of land.

Organization of Women in International Trade (OWIT) Kenya

An organization designed to promote women doing business in international trade by providing networking and educational opportunities (www.owit.org).

Methodological Note on Gender Inequalities and Economic Growth in Kenya

Theory suggests that economic growth is driven by the accumulation of capital and labor and by the productivity of these factors, which in turn depend on technology, efficiency, and institutions. Gender issues affect the way in which all these factors influence economic growth. There may be gender inequalities in the way that human capital is generated and in the distribution of physical assets such as land and capital. Gender issues may also influence technological progress, as well as the efficiency with which assets are employed to produce factor returns. Therefore, when women face disproportionate constraints in access to information, land, and capital versus their male counterparts or suffer from discriminatory access to education or labor markets, their productivity will be limited and their long-run prospects for economic growth will be adversely affected.

There are a number of methodological constraints in analyzing the link between gender inequality and economic growth. First, the importance of gender may not be directly measurable because the economic contribution of women (for example, childcare) may not be fully included in national income statistics (Blackden and Bhanu 1999). Second, some issues traditionally regarded as noneconomic have clear economic implications. Violence against women, cultural restrictions on the types of economic activities they can engage in, and intrahousehold dynamics regarding the ownership and control of resources strongly influence decision making within the household over the allocation of resources and their efficiency of use (Blackden et al. 2006).

Nevertheless, there is a growing theoretical literature showing that gender differences in education, employment, access to assets, and time burden have significant adverse impacts on economic growth. The main arguments from the literature are summarized below.

First, with respect to access to education, there may be a selection-distortion effect of gender inequality, adversely affecting growth performance. Less-able boys may be educated in place of more-able girls, lowering human capital in the economy. And if there are declining marginal returns to education, restricting education of girls to primary education while educating boys at secondary and tertiary levels implies that the marginal return to educating girls is higher and reducing inequality would improve growth rates (Knowles, Lorgelly, and Owen 2002).

Second, there are direct positive externalities associated with female education. There may be demographic effects such as lower fertility rates and reduced child mortality, which lower the dependency ratio and promote participation in the workforce while increasing savings. Female education has also been shown to promote the quantity and quality of education of their children, which raises future human capital and boosts economic growth (Lagerlöf 2003). This is particularly true for least-developed countries that remain in an equilibrium with large gender inequalities in female education, high fertility rates, low investment per child, and consequently low levels of per capita income (Blackden et al. 2006).

Third, gender inequalities in employment reduce the skill pool from which employers can hire workers and contribute to higher labor costs, thus lowering the competitiveness of the economy and reducing the potential for economic growth (Klasen and Lamanna 2003; Esteve-Volart 2004). Reduced disparities between male and female employment and earnings also increases the latter group's bargaining power within the household (Klasen and Wink 2002). This benefits not only the females concerned but also their children, who benefit from greater investments in health and education, thus improving the human capital of the next generation and their contribution to national income (World Bank 2001).

Fourth, inequalities in access to inputs distorts efficiency in that more-productive economic activities where women predominate (for example, agriculture) may be relatively underresourced versus less-productive male-dominated activities (Udry 1996; World Bank 2005b).

The fifth argument that gender differences have significant adverse impacts on economic growth relates to the time burden that women disproportionately face in household activities such as water and firewood collection and childcare. These time constraints reduce the ability of women to engage in market output, and therefore their total productivity is not captured in national accounts (Blackden and Wodon 2006). This is partly a measurement issue, but also an indirect growth linkage because the ability of households to maintain productive output depends on this unaccounted labor (Blackden et al. 2006). Female access to employment opportunities outside the home will lead to a substitution of unrecorded female labor in the household to recorded female labor in the formal economy.

Empirically, there is a body of cross-country evidence supporting some of these theoretical linkages. In particular, gender disparities in access to education have been shown to have a significant adverse impact on economic growth rates (Dollar and Gatti 1999; Forbes 2000; Knowles, Lorgelly, and Owen 2002; Klasen 2002; Yamarik and Ghosh 2003). Based on these empirical estimates, it is possible to determine an order of magnitude of possible growth effects for countries with gender inequalities in access to education. Klasen (1999) uses education spending as a share of GDP, intitial fertility levels, and changes in these as instruments for the levels of, and changes in, the female-to-male ratio of years of education. He concludes that gender inequalities have a significant and adverse impact on economic growth rates. For Kenya, Klasen (2002) shows that the fact that women during 1960–92 did not complete as many years of schooling on average as men did accounts for almost 1 percentage point difference between the long-run growth potential of Kenya when compared with that of high-performing Asian economies (with long-run growth rates of 4.5 percent).

Esteve-Volart (2000) examines the link between growth in GDP and gender inequality in primary schooling, using a sample of 90 countries and controlling for factors such as secondary education. The study shows that a 1 percent increase in the female-to-male primary enrollment ratio increases a country's growth rate on average by 0.012 percentage point. For secondary education, Dollar and Gatti (1999), using data for more than 100 countries, estimate than an increase of 1 percentage point in the share of adult women with secondary education increases per capita income growth, on average, by 0.3 percentage point. Applying the cross-country estimates of Esteve-Volart and of Dollar and Gatti to Kenya would imply the following:

- A year-on-year increase in the country's growth rate of 0.07 percentage point if the female-to-male primary school enrollment ratio were equalized (in 2004, Kenya's gross female-to-male enrollment ratio was 102:108)
- A year-on-year increase in GDP growth of 3.5 percentage points if female secondary education enrollment were brought up to the level of male secondary enrollment (in 2004, 482,000 boys enrolled in secondary education versus 431,000 girls—if 482,000 girls were enrolled, this would imply an increase in female secondary enrollment of 11.8 percentage points)

There is also some cross-country and cross-regional evidence that gender inequality in employment, in both access and type, similarly reduces economic growth (Klasen 1999; Klasen and Lamanna 2003; Besley, Burgess, and Esteve-Volart 2004). But unlike empirical investigations of the impact of gender inequalities in access to education, cross-country studies on the link between employment inequalities and growth suffer more from problems associated with data. Employment information is not easily comparable across countries, and there are potential endogenous issues in that growth may draw women into employment, not the other way around.

Microeconomic evidence indicates that gender disparities in access to productive inputs, such as land, fertilizer, seeds, and training, reduce the productivity of female farmers, and by more than the amount that inequality increases the productivity of male farmers (see Blackden and Bhanu 1999). Several studies have examined the relative productivity of men and women in farming in Sub-Saharan Africa. Saito et al. (1994) find that the gross output per hectare from male-managed plots is 8 percent higher than that on female-managed plots, while Moock (1976) proposes that if female farm managers in Kenya had the same access as men to extension services and productive inputs, their (maize) yields would be between 7 and 9 percent higher.

There is also evidence that the average production per farmer tends to be lower in countries where women represent a larger share of the agricultural labor force. In Sub-Saharan Africa, women are particularly disadvantaged when compared with men because they often farm smaller plots of land with more uncertain tenure. For Kenya, Quisumbing (1996) estimates that increasing female access to agricultural inputs to the same level as that of their male counterparts have would increase yields by 22 percent. Given the importance of agriculture in Kenya's GDP, this would translate into a one-off doubling in Kenya's growth rate from 4.3 percent (in 2004) to 8.3 percent. In 2004, Kenya's real production of crops was US$13.47 billion (2001 prices). Real GDP was US$14.05 billion in the same year, up from US$13.47 billion in 2003 (4.3 percent growth). A 22 percent increase in yields in 2004 would have implied a crop production of US$3.02 billion, increasing real GDP that year to US$14.59 billion (implying 8.3 percent growth over 2003).

It is important to interpret these figures with caution. While they are useful in identifying the magnitude of possible effects, they are not necessarily precise. In particular, there remain potential problems of causality with these types of analysis. If the positive relationship between gender equality and growth is caused by a two-way relationship or underlying common factor determining both simultaneously, then ordinary least squares regressions of income growth on measures of gender equality will be biased. This is particularly so when different variables pertain to the same period. Although studies have attempted to unravel the cause-and-effect relationship between gender equality and economic growth, these still run into problems of measurement and statistical inference. The most common technique is estimation using instrumental variables. This method identifies exogenous variables that directly affect gender equality, but not growth, and use measures of gender equality predicted from these variables as determinants of growth. For example, Dollar and Gatti (1999) use data on religion and civil liberties as variables that affect income only through their effect on gender equality in education. Klasen (1999) uses education spending as a share of GDP, initial fertility levels, and the changes in these variables as instruments for levels of, and changes in, the female-to-male ratio of years in education.

In addition, the limitations of microeconomic estimates must be noted. In particular, it is difficult to generate quantitative evidence on the efficiency effects of gender inequalities in access to land and inputs because men and women often collaborate on agricultural production by each providing certain inputs or they may produce different products, where once again it is difficult to disaggregate the growth effects of existing gender inequalities (Blackden et al. 2006).

References

ACEG (African Centre for Economic Growth). 2003. "Growth and Transformation of Small Manufacturing Firms in Africa: Insights from Ghana, Kenya and Zimbabwe." Nairobi, ACEG.

Adams, M. 2003. *Current Land Reform and Land Policy Processes in Kenya*. London: DFID.

AMWIK (Association of Media Women in Kenya). 2006. *The Dawn* (October 2005–January 2006).

Baden, S. 1998. "Gender Issues in Agricultural Liberalization." BRIDGE Report 41, Institute of Development Studies (IDS), Brighton.

Besley, T. 1995. "Property Rights and Investment Incentives: Theory and Evidence from Ghana." *Journal of Political Economy* 103 (5): 903–37.

Besley, T., R. Burgess, and B. Esteve-Volart. 2004. "Operationalizing Pro-Poor Growth: India Case Study." DFID, London.

Bevan, D., P. Collier, and J. Gunning. 1989. *Peasants and Governments: An Economic Analysis*. Oxford: Clarendon Press.

Blackden, C. M., and C. Bhanu. 1999. "Gender, Growth and Poverty Reduction: Special Program of Assistance for Africa, 1998. Status Report on Poverty in Sub-Saharan Africa." Technical Paper 428, World Bank, Washington, DC.

Blackden, C. M., S. Canagarajah, S. Klasen, and D. Lawson. 2006. "Gender and Growth in Sub-Saharan Africa: Issues and Evidence." Research Paper 2006/37,

World Institute for Development Economics Research, United Nations University, Helsinki. http://www.wider.unu.edu/publications/rps/rps2006/rp2006-37.pdf.

Blackden, C. M., and E. Morris-Hughes. 1993. "Paradigm Postponed: Gender and Economic Adjustment in Sub-Saharan Africa." Technical Note 13, Poverty and Human Resources Division, Africa Region, World Bank, Washington, DC.

Blackden, C. M., and Q. Wodon. 2006. "Gender, Time Use and Poverty in Sub-Saharan Africa." Working Paper 73, World Bank, Washington, DC.

Carr, M., ed. 2004. *Chains of Fortune: Linking Women Producers and Workers with Global Markets.* London: Commonwealth Secretariat.

Chemengich, M., and S. Gale. 2005. "Women and AGOA: An Analysis of the Impact of AGOA on Women in East and Central Africa." East and Central Africa Competitiveness Hub, Nairobi. www.ecatradehub.com.

Christie, I., and D. Crompton. 2001. "Tourism in Africa." Africa Region Working Paper 12, World Bank, Washington, DC.

Coetzee, G., K. Kabbucho, and A. Minjama. 2002. "Understanding the Re-birth of Equity Building Society." Equity Building Society, Nairobi.

Curry, J., M. Kooijman, and H. Recke. 1999. "Institutionalising Gender in Agricultural Research: Experiences from Kenya." Kenya Agricultural Research Institute, (KARI), Nairobi.

Cutura, J. 2006. "Voices of Women Entrepreneurs in Kenya." Report, IFC, Washington, DC. http://www.ifc.org/ifcext/enviro.nsf/AttachmentsByTitle/rep_GEMTools_VoicesKenya/$FILE/Voices+of+Women+Entrepreneurs+in+Kenya.pdf.

Ddamilura, D., and H. N. Abdi. 2003. "Civil Society and the WTO: Participation in National Trade Policy Design in Uganda and Kenya." CAFOD Trade Justice Campaign, CAFOD, London.

Dolan, C., M. Opondo, and S. Smith. 2002. "Gender, Rights & Participation in the Kenya Cut Flower Industry." NRI Report 2768, Natural Resources Institute, Kent, U.K.

Dollar, D., and R. Gatti. 1999. "Gender Inequality, Income and Growth: Are Good Times Good for Women?" Gender and Development Working Paper 1, World Bank, Washington, DC.

Ellis, A. 2004. "Why Gender Matters for Growth and Poverty Reduction." Draft, World Bank, Washington, DC.

English, P. 1986. "Where Does the Buck Stop?" In *The Great Escape? An Examination of North-South Tourism,* ed. E. P. English, chapter 2, 17–47. Ottawa: The North-South Institute.

EPZA (Export Processing Zones Authority). 2005a. "Annual Report for the Year 2005." EPZA, Nairobi. http://www.epzakenya.com/UserFiles/File/EPZ%20Annual%202005.pdf.

————. 2005b. "Horticulture Industry in Kenya 2005." EPZA, Nairobi. http://www.epzakenya.com/UserFiles/File/Horticulture.pdf.

Esteve-Volart, B. 2000. "Sex Discrimination and Growth." Working Paper WP/00/84, African Department, International Monetary Fund, Washington, DC.

————. 2004. "Gender Discrimination and Growth: Theory and Evidence from India." Discussion Paper, STICERD (Suntory and Toyota International Centres for Economics and Related Disciplines), London School of Economics, London. http://sticerd.lse.ac.uk/dps/de/dedps42.pdf.

FAO (Food and Agriculture Organization of the UN). 1989. *Report on the Global Consultation on Agricultural Extension*. Rome: FAO.

————. 1998. *Rural Women and Food Security: Current Situations and Perspectives*. Rome: FAO.

Feder, G. 1988. *Land Policies and Farm Productivity in Thailand*. Baltimore and London: John Hopkins University Press.

————. 2002. "The Intricacies of Land Markets: Why the World Bank Succeeds in Economic Reform through Land Registration and Tenure Security." Paper presented at the Conference of the International Federation of Surveyors, April 19–26, Washington, DC.

FIAS (Foreign Investment and Advisory Service). 2004. "Kenya: Improving the Commercial Legal Framework and Removing Administrative and Regulatory Barriers to Investment." FIAS, Washington, DC.

Forbes, K. 2000. "A Reassessment of the Relationship between Inequality and Growth." *American Economic Review* 90 (4, September): 869–87. http://web.mit.edu/kjforbes/www/Papers/Inequality-Growth-AER.pdf.

GJLOS (Governance, Justice, Law and Order Sector). 2005. "GJLOS Reform Update." GJLOS, Nairobi.

Government of Kenya. 1997. *Kenya Welfare Monitoring Survey III*. Nairobi: Central Bureau of Statistics, Ministry of Planning and National Development.

————. 1999. *National Micro and Small Enterprise Baseline Survey*. Nairobi: Central Bureau of Statistics, Ministry of Planning and National Development.

————. 2000a. "National Policy on Gender and Development." Nairobi.

————. 2000b. *Second Report on Poverty in Kenya, Vol. II*. Nairobi: Government Printers.

————. 2002. "Perspectives of the Poor on Anti-Poverty Policies in Selected Districts." Kenya Participatory Impact Monitoring, Human Resources and Social Services Department, Nairobi.

————. 2003a. *Economic Recovery Strategy for Wealth and Employment Creation 2003–2007*. Nairobi: Government Printers.

————. 2003b. "Kenya Country Commercial Guide FY 2003: Economic Trends." Central Bank of Kenya, Nairobi.

————. 2004a. *Kenya Review and Appraisal: Final Report on the Implementation of Beijing Platform for Action (Beijing + 10, 1994–2004)*. Nairobi: Ministry of Gender, Sports, Culture and Social Services.

————. 2004b. *National Land Policy Formulation Process: Concept Paper*. Nairobi: Kenya Ministry of Lands and Settlement.

————. 2005a. *Economic Survey 2005*. Central Bureau of Statistics, Ministry of Planning and National Development. Nairobi: Government Printers.

————. 2005b. "Kenya Gender Flier 2005." Department of Gender, Ministry of Gender, Sports, Culture and Social Services, Nairobi.

————. 2005c. "Medium Term Strategy 2005/2006 to 2008/2009." GJLOS Reform Programme, Nairobi.

————. 2005d. "National Land Policy Issues and Recommendations Report." Kenya Ministry of Land and Housing, Nairobi.

————. 2005e. "Sessional Paper No. 2 of 2005 on Development of Micro and Small Enterprises for Wealth and Employment Creation for Poverty Reduction." Nairobi.

————. 2006a. Ministry of Gender, Sports, Culture and Social Services Web site. http://www.culture.go.ke/.

————. 2006b. *Private Sector Development Strategy 2006–2010*. Ministry of Trade and Industry, Nairobi.

Horenstein, N. 1989. "Women and Food Security in Kenya." World Bank, Washington, DC.

Human Rights Watch. 2003. "Double Standards: Women's Property Rights Violations in Kenya." Human Rights Watch, New York.

Ikdahl, I., A. Hellum, R, Kaarhus, T. A. Benjaminsen, and P. Kameri-Mbote. 2005. "Human Rights, Formalisation and Women's Land Rights in Southern and Eastern Africa." Studies in Women's Law 57, Institute of Women's Law, University of Oslo (revised version of the Noragric Report 26, June 2005, Norwegian University of Life Sciences). http://www.jus.uio.no/ior/kvretten/kvrett_skriftserien/dokumenter/noradrapport.pdf.

Ikiara, M. 2001. "Vision and Long-Term Development Strategy for Kenya's Tourism Industry." Kenya Institute for Public Policy Research and Analysis, Nairobi.

Ikiara, M., and L. Ndirangu. 2003. "Prospects of Kenya's Clothing Exports under AGOA after 2004." Discussion Paper 24, KIPPRA (Kenya Institute for Public Policy Research and Analysis), Nairobi. http://www.kippra.org/Download/DPNo24.pdf.

ILO (International Labour Office). 2004. "Gender and Employment Dimensions of Poverty: Policy Issues, Challenges and Responses." National Policy Group, Policy Integration Department, Geneva.

Jacoby, H. G., G. Li, and S. Rozelle. 2002. "Hazards of Expropriation: Tenure Insecurity and Investments in Rural Chile." *American Economic Review* 92 (5, December): 1420–47.

Johnston, T. 2002a. *Domestic Abuse in Kenya*. Nairobi: Population Communication Africa.

———. 2002b. *Violence and Abuse of Women and Girls in Kenya*. Nairobi: Population Communication Africa.

Kenya Land Alliance. 2002. "Annual Report." Kenya Land Alliance, Nairobi.

Kimalu, P., N. Nafula, D. Manda, G. Mwabu, and M. Kimenyi. 2002. "Education Indicators in Kenya." Working Paper 4, KIPPRA, Nairobi. http://www.kippra. org/Download/WPNO4.pdf.

Kimenye, L. 1999. "Assessment of Technology Dissemination and Utilisation by Women and Men Farmers: A Case Study of Embu and Mbeere Districts." Proceedings of the KARI Gender Workshop on Institutionalising Gender in a National Research System, held at KARI Headquarters, Nairobi, October 5–8, 1998.

KIPPRA (Kenya Institute for Public Policy Research and Analysis). 2000. "Improving the Legal and Regulatory Environment for Business through Deregulation—Trade Licensing Reform." Ministry of Planning and National Development, Nairobi.

———. 2005. "Improving the Enabling Environment for Business in Kenya." KIPPRA, Nairobi.

Kirkpatrick, C., and D. Lawson. 2004. "Uganda Regulatory Cost Survey Report." Center on Regulation and Competition, University of Manchester, U.K.

Klasen, S. 1999. "Does Gender Inequality Reduce Growth and Development? Evidence from Cross-Country Regressions." Gender and Development Working Paper 7, World Bank, Washington, DC. http://siteresources.worldbank.org/ INTGENDER/Resources/wp7.pdf.

———. 2002. "Low Schooling for Girls, Slower Growth for All? Cross-Country Evidence on the Effect of Gender Inequality in Education on Economic Development." *World Bank Economic Review* 16 (3): 345–73.

Klasen, S., and F. Lamanna. 2003. "The Impact of Gender Inequality in Education and Employment on Economic Growth in the Middle East and North Africa." Background paper, World Bank, Washington DC. http://www.iai.wiwi. uni-goettingen.de/klasen/klasenlamanna.pdf.

Klasen, S., and C. Wink. 2002. "A Turning Point in Gender Bias in Mortality? An Update on the Number of Missing Women." *Population and Development Review* 28 (2, June): 285–312.

Knowles, S., P. K. Lorgelly, and P. D. Owen. 2002. "Are Educational Gender Gaps a Brake on Economic Development? Some Cross-Country Empirical Evidence." *Oxford Economics Papers* 54 (1, January): 118–49.

Lagerlöf, N. 2003. "Gender Equality and Long-Run Growth." *Journal of Economic Growth* 8 (4): 403–26.

Manda, D. 2002. "Globalisation and the Labour Market in Kenya." Discussion Paper 31, KIPPRA, Nairobi. http://www.kippra.org/Download/DPNo.31.pdf.

McCormick, D. 2001. "Gender in Small Enterprises in Kenya: An Institutional Analysis." In *Realising African Development: A Millennial Analysis*, ed. P. Samanta and R. Sen, 309–30. Kolkata, India: CIADS (Centre for Indo-African Studies), in collaboration with IIDS (International Institute for Development Studies).

Moock, P. 1976. "The Efficiency of Women as Farm Managers: Kenya." *Journal of Agricultural Economics* 58 (5): 831–35.

Ondieki, S. C., L. I. Mwarasomba, M. T. Hai, R. R. Thuo, and P. Mbogo. 2006. "Agrarian Reforms and Rural Development: New Challenges and Options for Revitalizing Rural Communities in Kenya. A National Report on Kenya." Presented at the International Conference on Agrarian Reforms and Rural Development: New Challenges and Options for Revitalizing Rural Communities, March 7–10, 2006, Port Alegre, Brazil. http://www.icarrd.org/en/icarrd_docs_nat.html.

Oostendorp, R. 2004. "Globalization and the Gender Wage Gap." Policy Research Working Paper 3256, World Bank, Washington, DC. http://www-wds.worldbank.org/external/default/WDSContentServer/IW3P/IB/2004/05/19/000009486_20040519163334/Rendered/PDF/wps3256globalization.pdf.

Owuor, E. 1999. "The Review of the Task Force on the Laws Relating to Women." Government of Kenya, Nairobi.

Quisumbing, A. 1996. "Male-Female Differences in Agricultural Productivity: Methodological Issues and Empirical Evidence." *World Development* 24 (10): 1579–95.

Randriamaro, Z. 2005. "Gender and Trade: Overview Report." BRIDGE. DFID, CIDA, and IDS, Brighton. http://www.bridge.ids.ac.uk/reports/CEP-Trade-OR.pdf.

Saito, K., H. Mekonnen, and D. Spurling. 1994. "Raising the Productivity of Women Farmers in Sub-Saharan Africa." Discussion Paper 230, World Bank: Washington, DC.

Schultz, T. 1991. *Research in Population Economies*. Greenwich, CT, and London: JAI Press.

Steyn, L. 2005. "Report on Progress with Monitoring and Evaluation Handbooks for LCBs/LDTs: Capacity-Building Programme for Kenyan Land Control Boards and Land Dispute Tribunals." Nairobi.

Strickland, R. 2004. "To Have and to Hold: Women's Property and Inheritance Rights in the Context of HIV/AIDS in Sub-Saharan Africa." Working Paper, International Center for Research on Women/Global Coalition on Women and AIDS, Washington, DC.

Thalman, D. 1997. "Report of Civic Education Study for Kenya Submitted to USAID-Kenya." World Learning, Washington, DC.

Thoen, R., S. Jaffee, and C. Dolan. 2002. "Equatorial Rose: The Kenyan-European Cut Flower Supply Chain." In *Supply Chain Development in Emerging Markets: Case Studies of Supportive Public Policy*, ed. R. Kopiki. Washington, DC: World Bank.

Transparency International-Kenya. 2003. "Women's Groups, Harambees, and Corruption: Pooling People's Wealth to Create Poverty?" *Adili* (50, December): 4–6. Nairobi. http://www.tikenya.org/documents/Adili50.pdf.

Udry, C. 1996. "Gender, Agricultural Production and the Theory of the Household." *Journal of Political Economy* 104 (5): 1010–46.

UMACIS (Uganda Manufacturers Association Consultancy and Information Services). 2000. "Uganda Regulatory Cost Survey Report." Report prepared for the Uganda Deregulation Project, Kampala.

UNDP (United Nations Development Programme). 2002. *Kenya Human Development Report 2001*. Nairobi: UNDP.

USAID (U.S. Agency for International Development). 2002. "Review of Gender Issues in the USAID/Kenya Integrated Strategic Plan (ISP) 2001–2005." Women in Development Technical Assistance Project, USAID, Washington, DC. http://www.usaid.gov/our_work/cross-cutting_programs/wid/pubs/kenya_gi_0900.pdf.

Wanjau, K., and V. Ndolo. 2003. "Challenges Kenyan SACCOs Face in Overcoming Regulatory Standards." CUTEA Regional Consulting Limited, Nairobi.

Were, M., and J. Kiringai. 2003. "Gender Mainstreaming in Macroeconomic Policies and Poverty Reduction Strategy in Kenya." African Women's Development and Communication Network, Nairobi.

World Bank. 2001. *Engendering Development through Gender Equality in Rights, Resources, and Voice*. Policy Research Report. Washington, DC: World Bank; New York: Oxford University Press. http://www-wds.worldbank.org/external/default/WDSContentServer/WDSP/IB/2001/03/01/000094946_010208053 93496/Rendered/PDF/multi_page.pdf.

———. 2003a. "Gender and Growth in Kenya: A Review of Evidence and Issues for the 2003 CEM." Chief Economist's Office, Africa Region, World Bank, Washington, DC.

———. 2003b. "Gender Equality and the Millennium Development Goals." Gender and Development Group, World Bank, Washington, DC.

———. 2003c. "Kenya: A Policy Agenda to Restore Growth." Country Economic Memorandum, World Bank, Washington, DC.

———. 2003d. "MENA Regional Development Report: Women in the Public Sphere." World Bank, Washington, DC.

————. 2003e. "Regional Program on Enterprise Development Survey." World Bank, Washington, DC.

————. 2004a. "From Periphery to Center: A Strategic Country Gender Assessment." PREM and ESSD, Africa Region, World Bank, Washington, DC.

————. 2004b. "Impact of International Trade on Gender Equality, The." PREM Notes 86, World Bank, Washington, DC.

————. 2004c. "Kenya: Enhancing the Competitiveness of Kenya's Manufacturing Sector: The Role of the Investment Climate." Investment Climate Assessment, World Bank, Washington, DC.

————. 2004d. "Republic of Kenya Country Assistance Strategy, The." World Bank: Washington, DC.

————. 2005a. "Kenya Financial Sector Adjustment Credit, Program Information Document." Report AB1567, World Bank, Washington, DC. http://www-wds.worldbank.org/servlet/WDSContentServer/WDSP/IB/2005/08/29/0001046 15_20050907093538/Rendered/PDF/KE1FSAC0PID0Appraisal0Stage.pdf.

————. 2005b. *Pro-Poor Growth in the 1990s: Lessons and Insights from 14 Countries.* Operationalizing Pro-Poor Growth Research Program, World Bank; Agence Française de DÉveloppement; Bundesministerium für Wirtschaftliche Zusammenarbeit und Entwicklung; and U.K. Department for International Development. Washington, DC: World Bank. http://siteresources.worldbank.org/INTPGI/Resources/342674-1119450037681/Pro-poor_growth_in_the_1990s.pdf.

————. 2006a. *Doing Business in 2006: Creating Jobs.* Washington, DC: World Bank and IFC.

————. 2006b. "Kenya Urban Informal Sector Investment Climate Analysis." Draft, World Bank, Washington, DC.

————. 2006c. "Republic of Kenya Country Social Analysis." Environmentally and Socially Sustainable Development, Africa Region, World Bank, Washington, DC.

Yamarik, S., and S. Ghosh. 2003. "Is Female Education Productive? A Reassessment." Photocopy, Tufts University, Medford, MA.

Index